The Lepchas of Dzongu Region in Sikkim

A Narrative of Cultural Heritage and Folklore

The Lepchas of Dzongu Region in Sikkim

A Narrative of Cultural Heritage and Folklore

by

Anita Sharma

INTACH

Aryan Books International

THE LEPCHAS OF DZONGU REGION IN SIKKIM
A Narrative of Cultural Heritage and Folklore

Text & Photography: Anita Sharma
Natural Heritage Division, INTACH

ISBN: 978-81-7305-443-3

Published in **2013** by

INTACH
The Indian National Trust for Art and Cultural Heritage
71, Lodhi Estate, New Delhi - 110003

and

Aryan Books International
Pooja Apartments, 4B, Ansari Road, New Delhi-110 002 (India)
Tel.: 23287589, 23255799; Fax: 91-11-23270385
E-mail: aryanbooks@gmail.com
www.aryanbooks.co.in

Computer Typeset and Printed in India at
ABI Prints & Publishing Co., New Delhi

Foreword

Tribal societies, located in the frontier regions, have not received adequate attention from scholars, perhaps due to their inaccessibility. The relatively few studies, although rich in material, are dated, having been undertaken much earlier. With growing accessibility the traditional mores, social organisation and traditional knowledge are fading away before the relentless advance of mainstream civilisation. Much, however, remains to be documented.

The Natural Heritage Division of INTACH has tried to address the knowledge gap and document the culture and social life of these tribes from an anthropological perspective by referring to the earlier studies and supplementing the same with fieldwork. The work has been ably carried out by the author, Ms. Anita Sharma, whose arduous efforts in the field and dedicated research have resulted in this serious contribution to the subject.

The work was supported by a modest grant from the Ministry of Culture, Government of India, during 2004-05. Rather than let the document crumble on some dusty shelf it was thought appropriate to put the material into the public domain.

Manu Bhatnagar
Principal Advisor
Natural Heritage Division, INTACH

Preface

Forces of modernity are fast transforming isolated societies. As the pace of change accelerates and draws them into the mainstream, there is need to understand and record their fast fading ways of life, traditions, culture, most of which are rooted in their deep relationship and understanding of their natural habitat.

The Lepchas are the original inhabitants of Sikkim, and recorded knowledge of the social and domestic life of these shy and retiring Himalayan people is scanty. The Lepchas of Sikkim, now in a minority, are concentrated in the Dzongu Reserve, north-central Sikkim, a region designated to protect their land and way of life. While they might appear insular to outsiders, studies reveal that their society is hardly stratified and amorphous within. Their age-old ethos of egalitarianism, good-citizenship and lack of aggressiveness combined with rich traditions and knowledge systems make them a fascinating subject for research.

Few scholars and travellers have attempted to map the Lepchas of Dzongu. Botanist J.D. Hooker authored the *Himalayan Journal* in 1875. Mainwaring compiled a Lepcha-English dictionary and a book on grammar (1876, 1885), Waddell analysed and documented the permeation of Lamaism into the Lepcha religion in 1899. The Lepcha society was originally studied in depth by Geoffrey Gorer in 1937. His exhaustive, if controversial, research has been of fundamental insight for almost every subsequent study done on the Lepchas, and this report is no exception. Arthur Foning, a Lepcha himself, also conducted a crucial study on his people in 1946. The National Museum of Denmark (Copenhagen, 1967) published anthropological studies conducted in Sikkim, Kalimpong and Git by Halfden Silger, from the Third Danish Expedition to Central Asia. Later, in 1989, Veena Bhasin examined the Lepchas of Dzongu and the Bhutias of Lachen and Lachung.

The Dzongu reserve is characterised by great environmental richness, diversity and beauty, and its geographical position has accentuated its isolation. During the course of history, the Lepchas came in contact with different races and were influenced by them in a number of ways. Though still a reserved area, the barriers are gradually fading. Today, with greater connectivity, implementation of government schemes and an enhanced economic status, the Lepchas of Dzongu are merging with the mainstream faster than was conceivable some years ago.

This report has been carried out for the purpose of recording the Lepcha society in transition under modern influences. Working under several constraints (time, inclement weather, resources and a shy subject), the report has managed to analyse and gather significant study material and update on the Lepcha life. The report's main value lies in analysing the impact of modernity upon their traditional society and the likely loss of oral knowledge in the areas of their socio-cultural patterns and knowledge systems. Their tradition in medicine and weather forecasting, hitherto unrecorded, have also been documented in the report. An attempt has been made to give greater voice to the Lepcha individual, who composes the larger society, and step away from the anthropological trend of studying societies where the individual is often ignored.

The Lepchas, in this report, have been addressed as both Lepchas and Rongs, or 'the people of the valley', as they like to call themselves. The fieldwork for this report was carried out from September to November in 2003, and the service of interpreters was often employed for the purpose of research. The primary source of data were the Lepchas of Upper Dzongu, and more specifically the inhabitants of the hamlets that comprise the Lingthem *busti*. Information was chiefly obtained by observation and interviews, and from secondary sources in the Teen Murti Library, New Delhi. This study would not have been possible without the unrelenting generosity and kindness of the Lepchas of Dzongu, and every member of Topden Lepcha's divine joint family. Chukmoo *azi* and Chuki stand out in memory for their constant gracious and indulging presence. Namgyal, Mika, OT and Chophel, of MLAS, the local NGO in Dzongu, were a great source of guidance and support. The Lepchas are indeed legendary hosts.

Anita Sharma

Contents

List of Illustrations

Fig. 1. Chendamu Lepcha and Den Tshering Lepcha.

Fig. 2. The Lepcha Reserve of Dzongu.

Fig. 3. Mangan, the district capital.

Fig. 4. Agricultural land.

Fig. 5. Lepchas worship the spirits of the mountains.

Fig. 6. A Lepcha household of Lingthem.

Fig. 7. The picturesque village of Tingvong.

Fig. 8. Every Lepcha inherits a putso affiliation from his/her father and must not marry in the same putso.

Fig. 9. All the Lepchas, young or old, know which putso they belong to.

Fig. 10. Remarriage is a common practice among the Lepchas after the death of the partner.

Fig. 11. Mun Sung Kun Lepcha.

Fig. 12. A typical picture of a nuclear family.

Fig. 13. Daughters do not inherit land and are involved in domestic work.

Fig. 14. Childern start participating in minor labour activities around the age of ten.

Fig. 15. The younger generation is hugely influenced by the Nepali and English languages.

Fig. 16. The Gompa society takes care of religious transgressions.

Fig. 17. A field of millet.

Fig. 18. Even picking fruits from a neighbour's tree is considered a wrongdoing among the Lepcha.

Fig. 19. *Lofit*–an essential accessory in Mun rituals.

Fig. 20. Young Lamas outside Lingthem Monastery.

Fig. 21. *Chotyens* at the Tholung Monastery.

Fig. 22. The Lingthem Monastery.

Fig. 23. Prayer flags are a common feature in Dzongu.

Fig. 24. Lama Yeshay Lepcha at the *sheda* in Lingzyah.

Fig. 25. Young Lamas.

Fig. 26. A giant prayer-wheel at the Tholung Monastery.

Fig. 27. Entrance of the Tholung Gompa.

Fig. 28. Bongthing Kenchoy Lepcha.

Fig. 29. With the coming of the Lamas the esteem of the Muns seems to have come down.

Fig. 30. Bongthing Natok Lepcha.

Fig. 31. With the death of the Muns their spirit seems to be dying as well.

Fig. 32. The Lepchas believe they originate from the people of Mayel.

Fig. 33. A man participating in ceremony.

Fig. 34. A thatched roof of bamboo and leaves given as an offering.

Fig. 35. A putso ceremony in Sankalang.

Fig. 36. A ceremony is performed for Tsang-dong, the god of the house.

Fig. 37. The birth ceremony is performed on the third day after a child is born.

Fig. 38. Objects traditionally buried with a dead body.

Fig. 39. Lepchas traditionally perform agricultural ceremonies to Sa Kya Rum twice every year.

Fig. 41. The Lepchas are gracious hosts.

Fig. 40. Lepcha men and women are very mild, polite and humble.

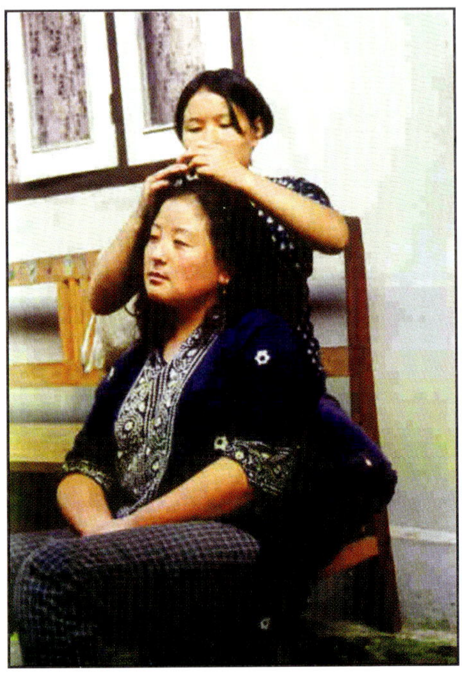

Fig. 42. Lepcha women command high respect.

Fig. 43. Families have now started sending their children to school.

Fig. 44. Cardamom plantation has improved the financial status of the people.

Fig. 45. Young girls are made to spend more time with parents than boys.

Fig. 46. Young Lepchas.

Fig. 47. The Dzongu has a strong language and literary tradition.

Fig. 48. The region is rich in biodiversity.

Fig. 49. The ancient literary works, known as Namthars, are recorded in Tibetan scripts.

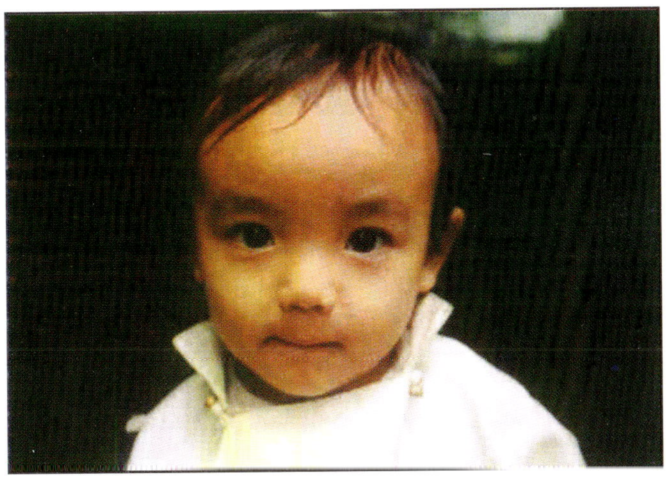

Fig. 50. Gaeythup Lepcha has been given a Lepcha name which means 'victorious'.

Fig. 51. The story of creation.

Fig. 53. Lepcha calendar.

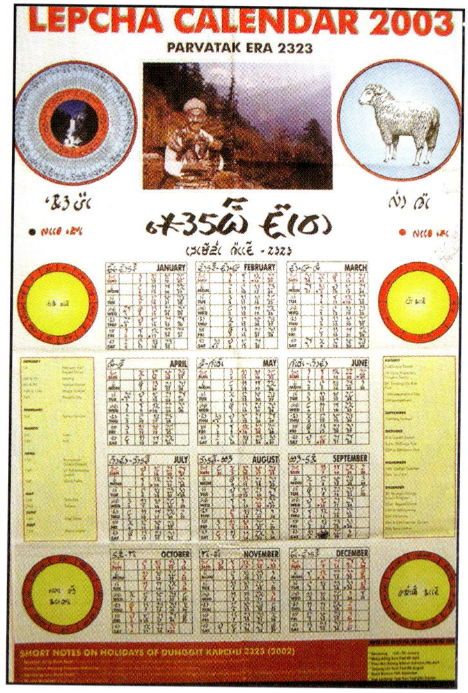

Fig. 52. The tale of two rivers.

Fig. 54. *Aee-ungpuh*, the honey container installed outside Lepcha homes.

Fig. 55. Medicine man Tshering Badur Lepcha.

Fig. 56. The primary health centre at Passingdang.

Fig. 57. Lama Apak Lepcha.

Fig. 58. The traditional Lepcha hat now gets a peacock feather.

Fig. 59. Traditional basket.

Fig. 60. Weaving is conventionally considered a woman's task.

Fig. 61. Traditional wood-carving.

Fig. 63. Traditional cane bridge.

Fig. 62. Cane bridge.

Fig. 64. Traditional dress of the Lepcha women.

Fig. 65. Fishing is practised as a leisure activity.

Fig. 66. Lepcha fruits.

Fig. 67. Leyap or simple gold or silver necklaces are common among women.

Fig. 68. Lepchas are known for their legendary love of music.

Fig. 69. The satsang, pali and tangbok.

Fig. 70. Traditional dance attire.

Fig. 71. A Lepcha house at Penang *busti*.

Fig. 72. A model Lepcha house at Namprikdang.

Fig. 73. The traditional Lepcha house made up of wooden logs, and elevated from the ground.

Fig. 74. The traditional Lepcha kitchen stove.

Fig. 75. Cardamom is the main cashcrop of the Lepchas.

Fig. 76. Children going to school.

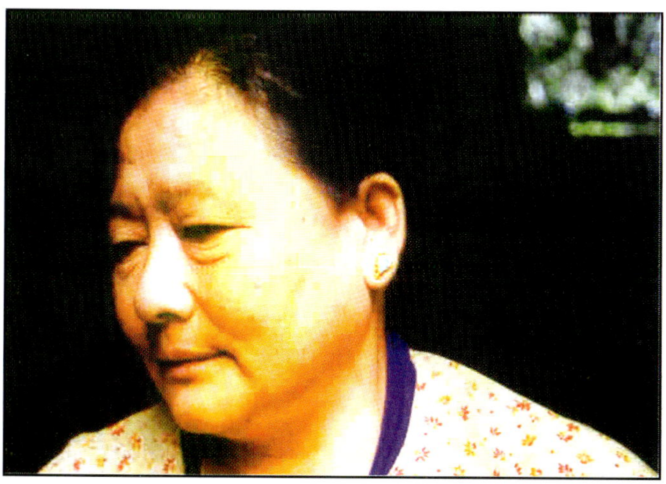

Fig. 77. Chukmoo Lepcha.

Fig. 78. *Mongku and korhuku.*

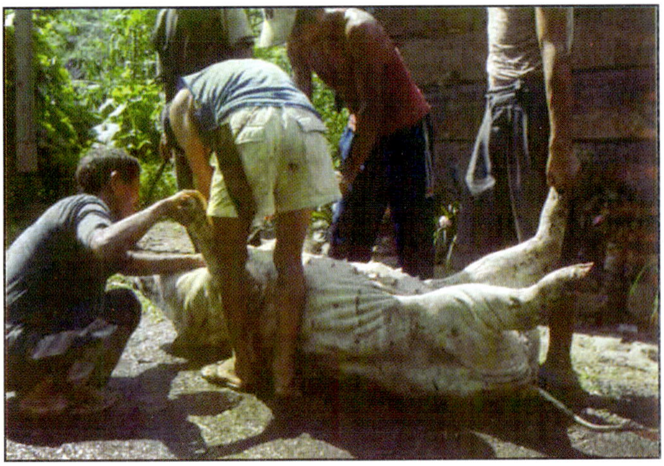

Fig. 79. Hunting as a regular occupation has declined.

Fig. 80. Turmeric drying in the sun.

Fig. 81. *Chi* is the favourite drink of the Lepchas.

Fig. 82. Traditional Lepcha kitchen.

Fig. 83. *Taling* and *takcham*.

Fig. 84. Beer is finding favour with the Lepchas.

Fig. 85. Lepchas of Dzongu are highly sensitive to nature.

Fig. 86. Prayer flags.

Fig. 87. The sacred lake at Heegyathang.

Fig. 88. Pastoral duties.

Fig. 89. A rare orchid.

Fig. 90. Relief: Tholung Gompa.

Fig. 91. Community meeting at Tholung Gompa.

LOCATION OF DZONGU

ADMINISTRATIVE BLOCKS OF DZONGU REGION

LOCATION OF SETTLEMENTS

ECO-TOURISM MAP OF DZONGU

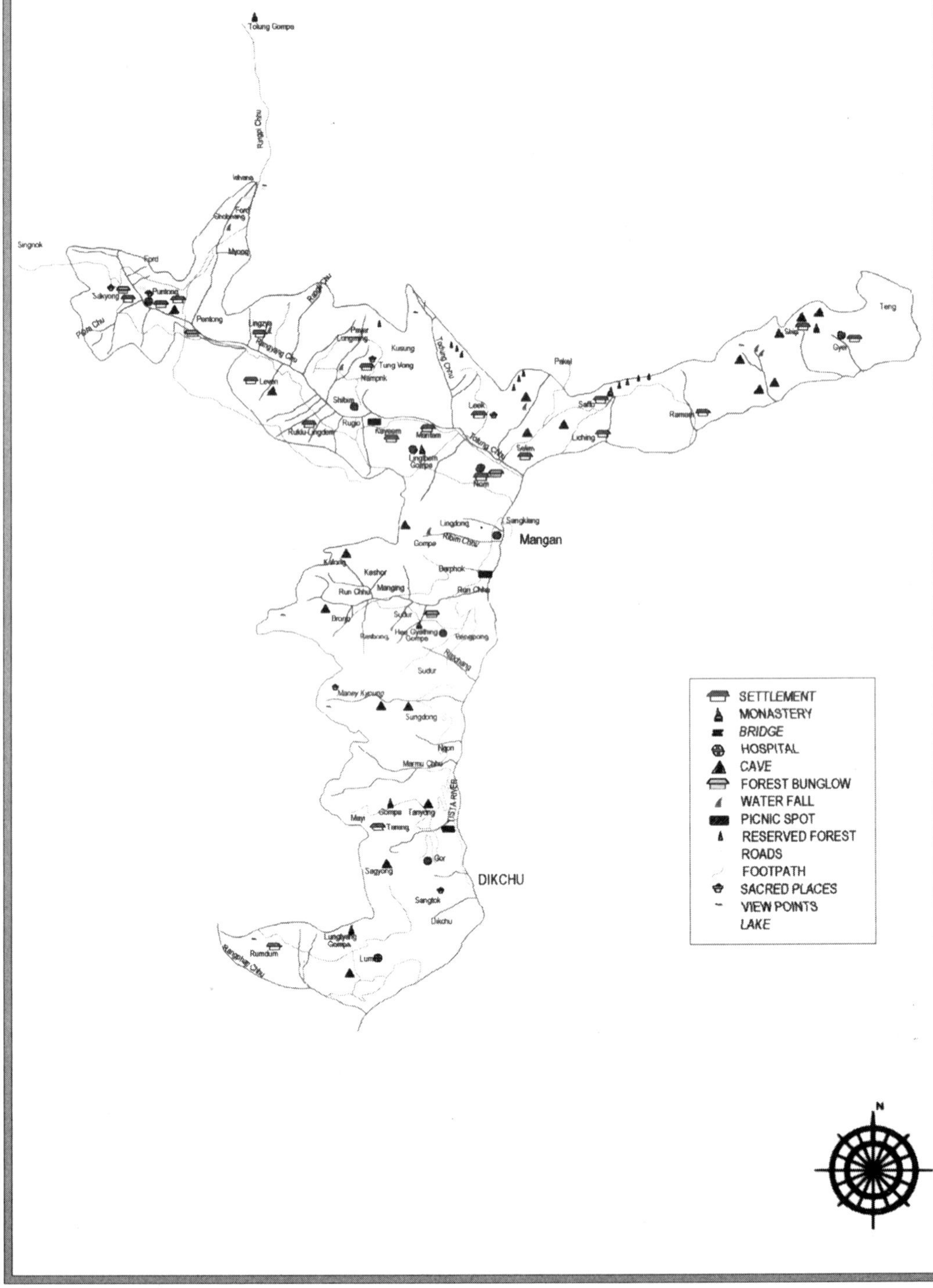

1

Introduction

The Lepcha Reserve of Dzongu in North-Central Sikkim has a population of 9,299 Lepchas, with 4,856 males and 4,452 females, in an area of 15,845.95 hectares.[1] However, the reserve also houses a shifting population of migratory Nepali labour who come here drawn to the lucrative cardamom trade.

The origin of the Lepchas is a topic of controversy among scholars. Historians and anthropologists are still debating whether the Lepchas originate from Naga tribes, or are associated with the Jimdars and the Mech in their eastward migration from somewhere in central Nepal. Some scholars have found similarities between the Lepchas and the tribes in Arunanchal Pradesh. Others believe that they are related to the Khasis of Meghalaya. The Lepchas, however, are content with the mythological explanation which traces them back to the kingdom of Mayal in an obscure valley around Khangchendzonga. However, there is evidence to show that the Lepchas have lived in this region from very early times. Most of the mountains, rivers and other prominent locales in Sikkim have Lepcha names, which also find prominence in the Lepcha folklore.

The Lepchas extend from Panakha in mid-Bhutan on the east into central Nepal on the west. They are divided into the Rong and Kambha tribes. The Lepchas call themselves Rong or the 'people of the valley'. This name was perhaps given to them by the Tibetans who addressed the people living on the mountain slopes as Rong-pa. Rongs are known to be shy and mild-mannered and perhaps, therefore, began to be called Lapchas after a submissive Nepali fish. This was subsequently modified into the English pronunciation of Lepchas. There is a proverb in Sikkim that a Lepcha is like a brass pot which can be used by all households. According to another version, the word Lepcha, derived from the Nepali language, can be translated as 'vile speaker' (Lap=speech, cha=unintelligible).

Local legend of the Lepchas has it that these people came from a mythological valley called Mayel that lies beyond the imposing peak of Khangchendzonga. It is believed that the Lepchas lived in their Mayel or paradise in a society that remained without stratification till the establishment of the monarchy by the migrated Tibetans in 1642, who later came to be known as the Bhutias.

A.R. Foning, a Lepcha, writes,

> The setup of our society is such that ranking and gradation is completely out of place; and it could be said with emphasis that there never has been any acknowledgement of authority save those of the seniors in our tribe. It can be asserted with equal emphasis that we Lepchas never had any king amongst us. Whatever kings we had and know of, were the Namgyal kings of the later evolved country of Renjyong or Sikkim carved out within our 'sanctum sanctorum', nay Mayel Lyang. The ancestors of these kings were installed in 1642 at Yoksam with our consent. This too was done because a few generations earlier, patriarch Tekung Tek, who was a Bonthing (priest of the indigenous religion of the Lepchas) but never a chief, as has been made out, was coaxed into ceremoniously swearing eternal friendship of brotherhood with the Tibetans who were gradually infiltering into our land.
>
> The person responsible for this vital task was Khye-Bumsa, the far-sighted and brilliant ancestor of the later kings. Eventually, as a result of this friendship pact, we agreed innocently to accept kings among us and we as a tribe have upheld them ever since.[2]

Before the planting of cardamom, there were no shops in Mangan and the Lepchas had to travel long distances in search of salt and other necessary goods. They used to barter minor forest produce and surplus crop, at the Tibetan border and established institutional friendship with Tibetans to convenience trading on the hazardous journeys. Later, the Lepcha-Bhutia alliance became prominent due to a common threat they perceived in the wake of the large-scale Nepalese immigration from the twentieth century onwards. Today, the Nepalese are the majority population in the state while Bhutias and Lepchas are a minority and have been granted tribal status by the government.

The district of Dzongu is a triangular, densely forested mountainous area with steep hill slopes. The area is fringed by the river Tista on the southeast and river Talung on the north-east. The mountains south of Khangchendzonga border the region on the third side. The land used for habitation and farming by the Lepchas of Dzongu is located on a relatively narrow strip above the two rivers, between 1,000 and 2,300 m above sea level. Above the farms lies the grazing land and forests, followed by the rhododendron woodland, after which begins the snowline. A prominent hilltop chorten stands opposite the junction of the Tista and Talung rivers from which narrow paths lead west and south to the different revenue blocks.

Dzongu is divided into 14 revenue blocks.

- Sakyong Pentong
- Tinbong
- Lingthem
- Barfok
- Gnon-Samdong
- Sangtok
- Ship Ger
- Lingzyah-Tolung
- Lingdem
- Lingdong
- Hee-gyathang
- Gor
- Lum
- Salim Pakhel

The district headquarters of Dzongu is Mangan, on the North Sikkim highway, which is subject to frequent landslides.

For this reason, till some years back the highway used to be open only a few months in the year. However, this had little impact on the lives of the locals who made the long and arduous journey to Mangan on foot. But today the situation has changed as the road is kept open throughout the year and the inhabitants of Dzongu no longer walk the distance to Mangan but use the daily morning jeep service to get to the district headquarters. Then again, it would be incorrect to assume that this odyssey has become a simple exercise. It is important to note that much of Dzongu continues to remain cut off from roads and the inhabitants of these areas have to walk for hours on end to reach the nearest road head to avail of the jeep service. The jeepable roads too are in a state of disrepair with long distances still uncarpeted, rendering them highly risky and difficult to manoeuvre at best. The maintenance of roads was given little impetus and the project has only picked up recently after 1983, a lag of about 20 years.

The locals segregate the reserve into Upper and Lower Dzongu. This separation is not so much the result of the altitude of the habitations, but the location of the sections situated on either bank of a tributary of the Tista that flows through the area. The section up to Barfok forms the boundary of Upper Dzongu while Lower Dzongu starts from Hee-gyathang.

The revenue blocks are further divided into a number of settlements or *busties*, with only one or two houses forming a *busti*, at times. The *busties* are scattered on the hill slopes, with houses often at considerable distances from each other interspersed with expanses of farms. Only a few locations have a cluster of a few houses. The *busties* of Lingthem and Hee-gyathang have the largest *gompas* or monasteries in the area and, more or less, act a focal point in the region. Smaller monasteries also exist in Samdong, Barfok, Pakyong, Leek and Sangtok. Small prayer wheels, or *maney*, can also be found in a number of *busties* of Dzongu.

Agricultural land is divided into different fields at varying altitudes. The house garden, or *sing*, stands in front of the house;

the wet paddy fields are situated at a lower altitude and temporary dry fields at a higher elevation. There is a shared land around the *busties* for grazing, pasturing and the collection of minor forest produce. The cardamom fields fall under tall shady trees. The burial and cremation grounds used by the Lepchas of Dzongu, lie at a considerable altitude from the *busties*.

The Dzongu region does not have any industry and the Lepchas, since long, depended upon the forest as their chief reservoir for survival against odds. The people here possessed a profound knowledge of the flora and fauna of the region, and believe that there can never be a shortage of food and resources for as long as the forests exist. Today, however, the Lepchas are mainly agriculturalists and more than 90% of the Lepcha households are engaged in cultivation. Cardamom has played a vital role in enhancing the economic status of the Lepchas of Dzongu and the presence of money, today, forms the fundamental economic basis in the lives of the Rongs. Lepchas are also increasingly earning their living through non-traditional methods like teaching, running shops and working in organisations and offices in Mangan. However, cardamom plantation predominates as the chief source of income for the Rongs of Dzongu.

The Lepcha society shows a strong patrilineal bias and is divided into different exogamous patrilineal *putso*, roughly translated as clans. The Lepchas continue to exist without a system of stratification and all *putso* are granted equal status. With the amalgam of Sikkim in the Indian Union, the Lepchas of Dzongu have adopted the popularly elected Gram Panchayat system that, to some extent, bears a resemblance to their indigenous one of Lyang-gambu or village elders. The shift to the Panchayat system is not a rupture of the indigenous governing traditions of the Lepchas, as the democratic village elder council has long been a characteristic of the Lepcha socio-political system.

The Lepchas speak the Rota, or Lepcha dialect and refer to their language as Rong-aring or Rongring. It is believed that before the coming of Lamaism, the Lepchas had a remarkable literary tradition of their own, but only a little of it seems to have survived the passage of time. Most of their ancient literary works, known as *Namthars*, however are now recorded in Tibetan script.

In ancient times, the Lepchas were nomadic and subsisted mainly on the collection of fruits, roots, tubers, leaves, fishing and hunting. They also practised primitive shifting cultivation aided by poor and simple technology. Today, the locals have moved on to a settled form of agricultural practice, only partially enhanced by gathering. Change was gradual, resulting in an interesting mix of influences both ancient and modern. Originally, the Lepchas were semi-animists and worshipped the spirits of the mountains, forests and rivers; perhaps a direct and natural outcome of their surroundings, later they integrated their indigenous religion with Lamaism. Today, however, they are under an increasing influence of the Nepali majority in the state, and a growing adoption of Western culture and mainstream Indian popular culture absorbed via glitzy popular media can be perceived. It is not uncommon today to come across young Lepchas in Dzongu, humming the latest Bollywood chart toppers. Some shifts may certainly be deciphered in the Lepcha psyche and society today. Even so, broadly, the Lepchas of Dzongu seem to have retained much of their fundamental ethos of simplicity, equality and joyful abandon.

2

Social Organisation

KINSHIP

The Lepcha language has a small number of kinship terms. They generally make no distinction in addressing their kin along maternal or paternal lines, the exception here being the mother's brother. The language also seldom acknowledges gender difference. Membership to a group is almost always along patrilineal descent. The son of a Lepcha is a Lepcha even if his mother is from another tribe. The Lepchas count nine generations back on the father's side and four on their mother's side, and address all cousins on the father's side as real brothers and sisters, and cousins' parents as real brother and sister-in-law of their father. The father's brother and father's father are allotted special respect and treated with utmost deference. The relationship of an individual with his/her parents-in-law is considered most delicate, especially between a man and his mother-in-law and a woman and her father-in-law, and the utmost restrain is observed while dealing with them.

Lepchas define kinsmen rather broadly and, defined strictly, the affines cannot be included in the kindred as they do not share common ancestry. Yet, the Lepchas treat in-laws like kinsmen who are potential reservoir of help. Today, however, the migratory Nepali labour force in Dzongu has considerably changed the traditional practice of communal labour in agricultural practices.

Marriage is seen as a transaction between kin-groups comprising whole families and not merely two individuals. A girl in the Lepcha household may not possess any transferable rights in her natal household but great emphasis is laid upon the affinal relations and their maintenance.

The levirate (the practice of marrying the widow of one's childless brother to maintain his line) and sororate (the custom of marriage of a man to his wife's sister or sisters, usually after the wife has died or proved sterile), are also practised. Sister-exchange marriages are not uncommon. The bond between the married daughter and her kin is maintained by frequent visits to her original *busti* and family. The girl's kin are also invited when the requirement of large *lobus* or aid-groups is felt. The matrikin are also important for strengthening *busti* ties. The *busti* persists as a social group with the knitting together of the agnatic and matrilineal bonds. Where such bonds lack, there exist no other structural ties to hold the society in a common bond.

Another interesting traditional practice was that of the would-be son-in-law working for his future in-laws. The prospective son-in-law's services could be availed for several years and a tendency to let go of the service on the father-in-law's part was often observed. This practice has almost ceased to exist in Dzongu today perhaps because it was found to be abusive and humiliating by the prospective grooms.

The implications of most Lepcha kinship terms seem to have remained unchanged from Gorer's time. Moreover, it is relevant to note that in spite of the widespread use of the Nepali language in Dzongu, the common terminology and medium to address the kin group is still the Lepcha tongue—with the exception of the commonly used *behani* and *daaju*, or sister and brother respectively, which I found was mainly used to address the migratory Nepali population in Dzongu. It may be observed that the Lepcha kinship system shows little digression from its traditional pattern and thus suggests its elementary role in the social organisation of the Lepcha society.

Putso or Clan/Caste System

The society of the Lepchas of Dzongu continues to exist without a system of stratification and all *putso*, roughly translated as clans, are granted equal status. The Lepcha society shows a strong patrilineal bias and is divided into different exogamous patrilineal *putso*. Every Lepcha inherits a *putso* affiliation from his/her father and must not marry in the same *putso*.

There is a difference of opinion behind the rationale of the creation of the *putso* among scholars. Perhaps *putso* was initially created to distinguish socially between different classes of Lepchas. In the times gone by, the Amzad *putso* that made agricultural implements was considered to be on a lower social rung as compared with the rest of the Lepchas. Today, however, the chief function of the *putso* is to convenience and regulate marriages. A Lepcha is not allowed to marry a member of his mother's *putso* up to four generations and up to nine generations on his father's side, thereby discouraging matrilineal cross-cousin marriages. There are a few 'original' *putso*, or caste/clan, among Lepchas called by the name of their dwelling place. The *Excerpts from a History of Sikkim* mentions 12 different clans among the Lepchas: Sengdong-mo, Lingsom-mo, Hee-mo—that further comprises Karthak-mo and the descendants of Thekong Salung. The rest are named after their dwelling places. The Lepchas of Dzongu, however, disagree with the above observation and claim to have numerous and not just 12 *putsos*.

Scholars also differ on the rationale behind the creation of the *putso*. According to Chattopadhyay, the Lepchas are divided into thirty-one "or so" sects or *gotras*.

> It was done on the same principle that gotras were created in the past in the remaining part of the country. However there were three major groups—Renzongmu or the inhabitants of Sikkim, Damsangmu, i.e. people of Kalimpong and Ilammu or those belonging to Ilam, now in Nepal.[3]

Gorer is of the opinion that the *putso* came into being because it stood for a geographical unit. He writes,

> ...in the very small villages there is a tendency for all, or at any rate the majority, of the men to be members of the same p(u)tso. But nowadays this has broken down (if indeed it was ever institutionalised) completely.[4]

Each *putso* is under the protection of certain spirits who are worshipped by the male members of the *putso*. These supernaturals are thought of as gracious and there seems to be no rivalry between the groups; but it may be observed that the guardian deity of the more populous *putso* is generally regarded as stronger. The advantage of belonging to a numerous *putso* being that there is a better chance of obtaining a second spouse if the first comes from a populous *putso*. Moreover, the people of the *putso* have a larger number of kin and, therefore, a larger number of people to turn to for help. However, taking their collaborative society into account, this advantage is clearly not an overwhelming one.

Gorer enumerates the function of the *putso* as such:

> Except as an exogamic classification the p(u)tso is now functionless... A traveller among strange people has no claim on the hospitality of the unknown members of his p(u)tso, though it would still be shameful for two members of the same p(u)tso to have sexual connection. More than anything else, the p(u)tso is a device for the prevention of incest.

Gorer's suggestion that the *putso* was perhaps a geographical unit has some interesting implications which he details,

> For with the p(u)tso as the geographical unit, the young men would have had no possible sexual partners except through adultery or incest; and, as numerous examples show, such situations inevitably lead to jealousy, fighting, and the splitting of the group. By their regulations, the Lepchas have reduced inter-group aggression to the minimum. The potential rivalry between father and son is mitigated by taking the arrangements for the child's marriage entirely out of the parents' hands; the potential rivalry between brothers is mitigated by allowing

younger brother access to his most favoured and stronger elder brother's wife, while making the relationship between an elder brother and his younger sister-in-law strongly incestuous. In this connection it is worthwhile noting that in the very large and elaborate Lepcha folklore and mythology I did not come upon a single instance of the otherwise almost universal compensatory story of the conflict between brothers, in which the despised, or ill-used younger brother or sister makes good after the elders have failed.[5]

During a Lepcha marriage ceremony, the girl's uncle says to her,

> You have been married into (the name) p(u)tso; now you are bound to them and if you had any other lovers you must leave them; now you have no connection with people other than this p(u)tso.[6]

It is of consequence to observe that even today, all the Lepchas, young or old, know which *putso* they belong to, and according to Gorer,

> A child should know who are his num-neu-zong, that is those people with whom all sexual contact is prohibited... By the time he is twelve or thirteen a boy should also know those women whom he is permitted to sleep with—usually a very much small number than those who are forbidden. In the case of those relations of a generation above his own—that is to say, the wives of his father's 'elder brothers', he also has to know, which of these women his father has slept with beforehand, for in that case the potential partner becomes permanently forbidden... Since sexual relationship outside the prohibited degrees is not considered embarrassing or important, no unpleasant or guilt-ridden situation arises...[7]

The Lepcha kinship organisation seems to have undergone little change in spite of the lapse of time since Gorer's study.[8] Perhaps this points to the fundamental nature of kinship in the social organisation of the Lepchas. The *putso* remains highly important even today and the traditional restrictions largely persist. One major change, however, is in the emphasis on monogamy among the Lepchas today. The impact of the outside world, not to mention the bombardment of popular monoculture via mindless programmes on television channels (especially Star Plus) and growing westernisation, has resulted in a generation of Lepchas who are ashamed of some of their conventional social and religious practices. Often, there is a tendency to disassociate themselves with their traditions and little effort is made to understand their true essence.

MARRIAGE

In the Lepcha tradition, marriages are not fixed directly by the parents of the girl and boy but with the help of go-betweens (*bek-bo*). However, the wishes of the parents and the girl and boy in question are also taken into account before the decision is made. Gorer highlights the role, or the lack, of the parents of the bride and groom in their marriage. He writes, "... the biological parents should have nothing at all to do with their children's marriages; were they to do so either the children would die or the marriage would break up."[9]

Spouses are generally chosen from other *busti*es, even in cases where larger *busti*es contain families from different *putso*s. This further helps to not only widen the social network of the Lepcha society but also to keep it well integrated. A Lepcha is not allowed to marry a member of his mother's *putso* up to four generations, and his own *putso*, which he inherits from his father, up to nine generations.

Marriage is the most important social ceremony and the most expensive one. Marriage ceremonies are important social events where relatives and friends from near and far come to participate in the occasion. The ceremony is funded by the groom's father and is held in the boy's parents' home. Traditionally, the Lepcha marriage is believed to have seven stages with the most important being *asek* or betrothal, and bringing the bride home or *bree*. Wedding ceremonies (described in detail by Gorer and what's more, the atmosphere compared to 'an English pub') went on for a period of two days and one night, and were generally supervised by an elderly *Mun*. Today, however, marriage ceremonies last only for a night and are consecrated by a *Mun* and a Lama or, in some cases, only by a Lama. This is clearly another indication of the diminishing importance of Lepcha priests and the dominant status of the Lamas in Dzongu today.

The levirate (the practice of marrying the widow of one's childless brother to maintain his line) and sororate (custom of marriage of a man to his wife's sister or sisters, usually after the wife has died or proved sterile) are also practised, though monogamy is the general rule. Sister-exchange marriages are not uncommon either.

Traditionally, a man possessed sexual rights with his elder brother's wife. Here the brother could be real or classificatory. A Lepcha could also inherit the wives of all his younger uncles, from both the mother and father's side, and all younger sisters of his wife.[10] Gorer claimed that the Lepchas wholeheartedly enjoyed such rights and the younger brothers shared the burden of the bride price.[11] In case the wife proved to be sterile, the husband was allowed to demand a second wife from his wife's family. Today, however, most Lepchas claim that their sexual rights are only limited to their spouses and their ancient practices have been discontinued. This is observed to be largely true although some deviances might exist in the remote parts of Dzongu.

It is customary for a widow to be inherited by the dead man's younger brothers, preferably the next in succession. If that is not possible then the widow may also be taken in by the nephew. The man in question, however, may already have a wife. Nevertheless, this ensures that the family property stays within the family and in cases where the widow has sons, she can continue to live in her husband's *busti* without having to marry any other male member of the family, as the sons have the customary right to property.

If a widow wishes to marry outside of her husband's *busti*, the groom in question has to pay *asek* (the bride price) to her late husband's *putso*, as according to the Lepcha tradition the wife is purchased by the husband's group so she continues to be the property of her husband's *putso* even after his death. This can be underlined by the fact that a widow may be remarried to another member of her husband's *putso* even without consulting her parents. In theory, she does not possess the rights to refuse a match fixed by her husband's *putso*, but if she does so then her *putso* has to supply another girl in her stead without the bride price. Similarly, if the man refuses to marry the woman in question, he has to supply another man in his place. However, in practice these incumbents are not followed. In cases when a woman remarries outside of her husband's *putso*, the bride price has to be paid to her husband's *putso*. In a family, the individual will is considered inferior to the collective will.

The husband of a dead wife has to carry a pig and *chi* to her parents' house on the 49th day after her death. It is customary for the parents of the dead wife to offer a younger sister of his deceased wife to the husband. If he expresses the wish to not accept the offer of the younger sister, he traditionally has to present an ox or a pig, *chi*, grains and money, to be relieved of the obligation.

A boy's marriage is a great financial burden and is sometimes beyond the means of the boy's parents. In the Lepcha household, where every hand counts the boy's marriage also has emotional and economic repercussions, so it perhaps may be assumed that there is some resistance to marry the son from the parents' side. This view, however, will be denied by the Lepchas but statistics do support this point. The Lepchas claim to marry early, but in reality, a large number of men are not married till the age of 30. The number of widows, widowers and divorcees are almost non-existent and perhaps stress the absolute need of optimum labour use and the position of women in the society. It is, in fact, a difficult economic setback for parents to lose their children's labour, give them their share of property and fund their marriage. Moreover, traditionally, this also indicates a certain loss in the status as head of the family as the married son automatically becomes more prominent with the family he starts.

A few changes can be deciphered in the marriage system of the Lepchas. Dr. Gyamtso Bhutia, the only doctor in Dzongu, claims that the incidence of teenage marriage is considerably lower. This is a major shift from Gorer's time in the reserve in the 30s, who recorded that in Lingthem, there were only four unmarried girls over the age of twelve.[12] The incidence of teenage marriage has come down. A new type of marriage or *lungtitchihit* (marriage by elopement) is also observed and, in fact, common among the Lepchas today. The popularity of such a marriage is perhaps because it involves far lesser expenses as compared with the traditional marriage. The first such marriage was recorded in the 1960s. The practice of *lungtitchihit* has also resulted in the diminishing role and status of the *bek-bu*. Otherwise, marriage continues to proceed in the stages of *asek* and *bree*, although the period between the two has reduced, and *bree* is followed only after a month's time by *asek*, and not years, as was the traditional practice. The economic cost of a traditional marriage is considerably low today as well. The appearance and age of a potential spouse is now also an important consideration in marriages and not just the traditional observations of the individual's character and property. I was also told that a history of leprosy and perjury is another important consideration in marriages.[13]

The different types of marriages prevalent among the Lepchas are:

- Kampho – *asek* is paid after the marriage takes place immediately.
- Achoktying – this marriage is spread over a period of three years not common among the Lepchas today.
- Marriage by service – the would-be has to work with his in-laws to reduce *asek* price. This system of marriage is rarely seen in Dzongu today.
- Lungtitchihit – marriage by elopement is common among the Lepchas today.

- Marriage by exchange – two siblings of one family marry two siblings of another, thereby equalising the bride price.

Both men and women in Dzongu openly condemn polygamy today. This is perhaps a result of influences from the outside world, including education and the disappearance of sterility from Dzongu. Sterility was a big issue in Dzongu and the Lepchas here suffered from a dangerous venereal disease, locally known as *tanji*, which is believed to have spread in the area in the end of the 19th century. Some of the Lepchas rendering free labour to the king across the Indo-Tibetan border are said to have contracted the infection from prostitutes on the trade route. This disease caused widespread infertility among the Lepchas and was eventually eradicated from the reserve in 1959, by a medical team headed by Dr. Shanti Gopal Sinha and sponsored by the Indian government. It is speculated that *tanji* plagued the population growth of Dzongu for about 70 years and is perhaps responsible for the low population of the Lepchas until today.[14] To my surprise, none of the medical officials appointed in Dzongu, including the only doctor in the reserve, Dr. Bhutia, were aware of this medical history. Widespread sterility is alluded to as a chief rationale behind the practice of polygamy in Dzongu. Sterility has thus worked as a fairly significant dynamic in shaping the social organisation of the Lepchas of Dzongu.

The young generation of Lepchas today seems to have readily adopted some mainstream Hindu viewpoints on marital relations. A gentleman in his early 30s, whose name I prefer not to reveal, vehemently conveyed his disgust with their traditional practice of holding conjugal rights with the brother's wife. He rounded up his thoughts with the revealing Bollywood favourite "*bhabhi to maa ke samaan hoti hai*" or, "the brother's wife is like a mother". The wind of change is indeed sweeping these placid Himalayan folk away from their roots and often replacing their sense of pride with insecurity and shame in their indigenous practices. Perhaps, more than ever before, it is relevant to understand the true connotations behind these traditions before any such judgement is hastily passed.

Chattopadhyay's words provide some food for thought:

> In this custom what escapes their notice is the social wisdom of remaining non-possessive and non-aggressive about a thing people are generally most possessive and aggressive about. This is just an instance. Before any such customs are given a go-by under pressure from a culture which cannot still eradicate wife-beating, suttee or bride-burning, serious thoughts are necessary. On the contrary, a social more which eschews violence, aggression, jealousy and rancour cannot be considered retrograde.[15]

FAMILY

The nuclear family is the smallest and most important unit of the Lepcha social organisation. It is the economic as well as the participatory unit in all social, religious and public endeavours. The predominant type of families here are either nuclear or joint. The nuclear family generally has its own separate residence with the eldest son inheriting the father's house. Some families consist of three generations—old parents, the eldest son, his wife and children. If the older parents stay with the son, they are incumbent to work in his fields and receive food from him. The role of the head of the family is gradually transferred to the eldest son from the father.

A nuclear family may, for a time, include an individual who joins in the economic activity of the family. A daughter lives with the husband's family after marriage and does not possess any rights of inheritance in her father's property. However, there have been instances of daughters inheriting land and property from the father but these are based on individual discretion and are more an exception than a rule among the Lepchas. After marriage, sons traditionally remain in the *busti* with their families, but tend to increasingly achieve greater social and economic independence. Many are also observed to be throwing in their lot in Mangan and Gangtok. Yet, it would not be incorrect to say that the sons do not achieve absolute independence from their families at least until the father is alive.

Most households are a farming unit and subsistence from agriculture provides the *busti* with its chief economic life. The family tries to get the maximum out of each individual and optimise on adult labour to cater to the scattered fields that the Lepchas possess. Labour is maximised by birth, marriage, adoption and incorporation. When a wife is infertile, polygamy is the means to obtain an heir. A widow is provided with a husband through polygyny (through the mechanism of fraternal inheritance). This also helps to retain her labour and avoid separation of families for the children. Incorporation of young male relations and would-be sons-in-law are other means to supplement the labour force of the family unit. However, these dynamics have been somewhat altered by the ready availability of Nepali labourers in Dzongu today.

Children start participating in minor labour activities around the age of 10. The distribution of authority and labour in a family exists but is highly flexible. Each family has a recognised head who represents the family in various matters. A woman is regarded the chief representative of the family only in the complete absence of a male adult. However, in the confines of the nuclear family, men and women are considered more or less equal, with decisions being mutually taken by both the partners.

All these measures serve to maintain the family unit of the Lepchas as a viable and independent element of the larger social group, supplementing its labour force by external induction if the need arises.

Division of labour

Labour is divided in a household chiefly on the lines of sex and age although it is not rigid in nature. The tasks that need to be performed can be grouped into broadly two categories.

- Domestic work – cooking, cleaning and washing is performed mainly by the female members of a family.
- Agricultural work – shared by men and women except that ploughing is carried out exclusively by men. On the other hand, men provide wood and water for the house and also cook on occasions.

Inheritance

There is no legal will in the Lepcha society. In the traditional system, *ringtham* (Ring = speech, Thing = a matter or thing) is the verbal declaration made by an individual before his death regarding his property and debts. The property is divided equally among the sons. Daughters do not inherit land but may share animals and jewellery. In case the daughter possesses *athyel* land, or the land given to her by her parents, she can continue to cultivate, or use the land for a few years after marriage if her parents are alive, but she does not own the land. But livestock given on *athyel* can be inherited by her.

A family with no male heir may leave his property to his younger brother or nephew or take a resident son-in-law who can thus inherit his property. But this is not favoured by the Lepchas perhaps because the property then moves out of the *putso*. Adopting a child is a more favourable option, though the father has to seek permission by the village elders to adopt a child. Adoption usually takes place when the child is between the age group of three to seven. A pig was traditionally slaughtered for the occasion and the mother of the child was gifted with the sacrifice and a new set of clothes.

Family: formation and change

The Lepchas do not split their families. However, if a family becomes too large and does not agree on vital issues, then it may split up into small units and the property divided with the supervision of the Panchayat.

Among the Lepchas, all the land and property are registered in the name of the head of the family. Traditionally, when the son and daughter were around 10 years old, they were given a small piece of land and small implements to cultivate their little patch of property. Girls were usually given animals that they cared for and could save the earnings for dowry. A girl is allowed to take the animals to her husband's house after marriage. With the growing emphasis on education, such practices are less common in Dzongu today.

Additional areas are given to the boy as he grows up. But the earnings from his land can be spent by him or his parents. The parents start preparing for the division of property in their lifetime though the substantial splitting of land only takes place after the parents die or the property is split up in their lifetime. The tradition of *athyel*—splitting of the parents' property while they are alive—attributes to the setting up of the married couple in a separate house.

A family's landholdings in the Dzongu reserve are often distributed among several fields which may be widely separated owing to the topographical nature of the area. This creates the problem of a large amount of travelling time between the home and the fields and it might be difficult for a small nuclear family to maintain a normal existence. Hence, the help of seasonal labour is often sought and any additional help from outside is always welcome. In a joint family, if the fields are far away, a son may permanently shift to the field house in the distant farmland with his family. But they continue to remain a part of their *busti* and continue to attend all the important religious and social activities of the *busti*.

A *busti* may also be divided into smaller units if it is found too large to be easily manageable. The idea behind regrouping of a *busti* is to maintain a certain amount of independence and self-sufficiency for the *busties'* smallest unit—the family.

Socio-Cultural Biography

SOCIO-POLITICAL SYSTEM

The Lepcha society shows elements of what is known as a 'kinship society' as opposed to a 'market dominated society'. But the Lepcha community differs from a kinship society as there are no inharmonious traits overwhelming the socio-political system that are prevalent in the kinship system. Being largely unstratified, it can be said that the indigenous system of power and status in the Lepcha society is based on relative egalitarianism and democracy. With the amalgam of Sikkim in the Indian Union, the Lepchas of Dzongu have adopted the popularly elected Gram Panchayat system that, to some extent, bears a resemblance to their indigenous one of Lyang-gambu or village elders. Therefore, it would not be incorrect to say that the shift to the Panchayat system is not a rupture of the indigenous governing traditions of the Lepchas, as the village elder council has long been a characteristic of the Lepcha *busti*es. The elimination of the powerful offices appointed during the monarchy and, conversely, the introduction of the council Kyoung Shezum or *Samaj* also points towards the continuing practice of their native democratic traditions merged with the adopted Indian system.

The Lepchas have the following village government bodies:

- Busti Panchayat
- Gompa Society
- Mandal Committee
- Gyapon
- Youmi
- Mukhtiar
- Lyang-Ganbu (village elders)
- Kyoung Shezum or Samaj or Society members

Busti Panchayat

The Panchayati Raj Act was implemented in the state after Sikkim's incorporation with India and the socio-political system of the Lepchas of Dzongu is gradually changing to conform to it. Under the Act, the administrative control of the *busti*es is vested in a *busti* or Gram Panchayat elected by all the adults of the *busti*. There are seven Panchayat blocks in Dzongu, two in Lower Dzongu and five in Upper Dzongu. Each block has a popularly elected Panchayat which is run by a President, Vice President, Secretary, a *Zila* Member and five other representatives. The Panchayat meets every month to discuss the impending key matters. The last elections in Dzongu were held in November 2002. Till the 80s, the government gave the Panchayat only a sum of Rs. 130 for stationary supplies, annually. All the other expenses were met by the members of the Panchayat.[16] This has been amended today as the Panchayat now receives Rs. 3-4 lakhs from the government and there is an indication of further increasing the sum to Rs. 10 lakhs annually, from 2003.

This fund is utilised for expenses on water and sanitation, small-scale industry, ICDS or Integration of Child Development Society and forest plantation, among other necessary undertakings. The inter-*busti* paths, log-bridges, construction of public buildings and Gompa path-clearing work is carried out by the Panchayat. *Ohlok*, or collective labour, is arranged for communal work and one member of each household of the *busti* is summoned by the Gyapon for the purpose. The Panchayat members possess the right to fine a small sum of money and a bottle of liquor from an individual found to be absent from the Ohlok, but this is not commonly exercised by the Panchayat today. The right to demand liquor as fine from an individual is also not in practice anymore. It is of consequence to point out that there is a growing emphasis to reduce the impact of alcohol by the socio-political councils in Dzongu today.

Gompa Society

Each *busti* has an elected Gompa Society, headed by Tuhik and Gumbyapan or the head Lama. Once elected, these two members become permanent representatives while four or five members are elected from the concerned *busti*es every three to five years. There is no criterion of age in this membership. The function of these elected members is to collect tax from vendors and maintain income accounts during fairs and festivals. The accounts are checked by the head Lama who can also allocate the finances towards the repairs and maintenance of the monastery. Together, the Panchayat and Gompa Society form an inquiry commission and can fine a troublemaker found guilty of disrupting the law of the land.

Mandal Committee

The Dzongu reserve was the private estate of the royal family of Sikkim. The chief administrator was the Kazi who lived outside of Dzongu and controlled the region through subordinates known as Mandals. Dzongu was divided into 12 blocks with a Mandal heading each unit. The office of the Mandal was created at the beginning of last century, as earlier the Lepchas could gather food without any official permission. The office of the Mandal was hereditary within the extended

Lepcha family. The Mandal was recognised as the landlord of the villages while those who lived in it were spoken of as his tenants. The chief duty of the Mandal was to maintain village affairs and collect revenue for the royal court. The Mandal was regarded with substantial esteem and helped the villagers in organising marriages and arranging feasts, among other things. Prior to 1940, the Mandal also possessed the right to confiscate land if outstanding taxes were not paid within a period of two years. The seized land was handed over to the Kazi who gave the Mandal a commission of 5% in return. The Mandal could also grant a reduction of house and land tax, and could demand three days of free labour annually from every household. If a person failed to pay his taxes, the Mandal would help him to arrange a feast where all the guests would contribute to help the host and bail him out of trouble. The Mandal was an important official during the monarchy. Gradually, after the adoption of democracy, however, the Mandal's sway was reduced considerably and he became a representative who collected the annual tax for which he received 10% commission. Other duties of the office of the Mandal were transferred to the Panchayat. The office of the Mandal was annulled in 1987, and is no longer in existence today.

Gyapon

The Gyapon is elected in turn from each family in the *busti* for a period of three years. He was traditionally the mediator between the Mandal and the *busti* folk. He was responsible for collecting tax, gathering villagers for community work and prevention of crime and disputes. The office of the Gyapon had no privileges but he commanded considerable respect, as the only motivation of the officer-in-charge was to serve the people. Today, the Gyapon collects money from farmers on forest-wood used for agriculture and hands over the collection to the forest department. Gyapon is a Sikkimese-Tibetan word, but today the Nepali term *karobari* is also in use.

Youmi

Linguistic evidence illustrates that the office of the Youmi predates the above official posts. It is a Lepcha word with no equivalents found in the Sikkimese-Tibetan tongue. Youmi are wise old men who traditionally assisted the Mandal in the village affairs. Today, the Youmi mainly passes orders to the Gyapon to collect money from the villagers and assists the Panchayat in their endeavours. Youmi is usually an ex-Gyapon and a *busti* may have more than one Youmi. Besides the prestige of the title, the Youmi gets no material advantage from the post. Traditionally, in case of the death of a Mandal without an heir, the next Mandal was chosen from the Mandal's clan or *putso* and the Youmi would act as the officiating Mandal until the selection of the new Mandal was confirmed.

Mukhtiar

The office of the Mukhtiar was introduced in the area at a later stage. Two Mukhtiars were appointed for the Dzongu reserve. They were superior to the Mandal and handled their revenue accounts and maintained the birth and death register. The Mukhtiars paid impromptu visits to farmlands to access the freshly sown farms, as the tax was charged on the seeds grown and not the produce. The Mukhtiar was empowered to charge a higher fine from the villagers as compared with the Mandal. These officials were responsible for the maintenance of order and the regulation of intra-*busti* affairs in Dzongu. The office of the Mukhtiar is no longer in existence today.

Lyang-Ganbu (Village Elders)

The Lyang-ganbu or village elders act as an informal advisory council to the Panchayat and the *busti* people at large. They try to resolve issues that become a matter of dispute and have not been solved by either families or their *putso*. This informal council may be formed spontaneously with the congregation of the senior and elderly members who happen to be present at the point, or after the summoning of the respected men of the locality. These men discuss the problem at hand and try to find a solution. If the outcome is not acceptable to both the parties concerned, then it is referred to the Panchayat. But, this happens only on rare occasions. The inter-*busti* disputes are taken to the Panchayat. Disputes are observed to be on a gradual rise today, and the main reason cited for this shift by the Lepchas is the increase in the number of Nepali migrants. Clashes between brothers are also on the rise. If the verdict of the Panchayat is not acceptable to the disputing parties, the matter is taken to the Mangan court.

Kyoung Shezum or *Samaj*

Kyoung Shezum or *Samaj* members are also called Society Members in Dzongu. This is an informal council of young people who help clear disputes and matters pertaining to crime. They also act as social workers in case of disasters and adversity like the death of a member of the *busti*. Kyoung Shezum is a new introduction to the socio-political system of Dzongu, and is reported to have been introduced here in the late 80s. The creation of Kyoung Shezum perhaps points to the growing initiative and empowerment of the young generation in Dzongu. Another interesting aspect of this newly introduced system of governance is that it has a synonymous term in Nepali as well as in English: Samaj or Society members. These terms appear more in use than their Lepcha counterpart. Perhaps, this could also be an indication of the growing influence of the two languages especially among the young.[17]

COMMUNITY LIVING

The Lepcha society has a fine network of labour groups based on the principle of mutual exchange, and this exchange of assistance is common to the Lepcha everyday life. Each family is a part of these mutual help groups. The assistance is well reciprocated by the Lepchas and is, indeed, seen as an investment. It is interesting to note that none of these mutual aid groups are based along *putso* or kinship lines. Extended families may be extremely important, but in day-to-day matters, it is these mutual aid-groups that are relied upon. This also enumerates how obligations to the family, *busti*, public institutions, neighbours, aid-groups and friends act as the paramount force that unites the community and connects the family unit to a larger group or community. Giving and receiving of hospitality are the major binding factors of the Lepcha society. To remain a part of this community, however, an individual or family must be willing to host feasts for the entire village on important social occasions and partake in other events of the *busti* life.

The Lepcha society has in practice the following mutual aid-groups:

- Lobu
- Lyangcho
- Ochhom
- Ohlok

Lobu

The relaxed and comfortable bonds of friendship and neighbourliness may be recognised by what is known as a *Lobu*. A *Lobu* is a person who is asked for help, and when his aid is returned, it is called *nglok* (repaying debt). Each family is a part of a long-term *Lobu* group which includes family members, neighbours and friends, tied together by their residential propinquity or the geographical location of their farmlands. A person can be a member of one or more *Lobu* groups. This system tends to take place between families and not just an individual, and the obligations are often passed from father to son.

All *Lobu* members are expected to give gifts and their personal labour in times of important social events or need, like construction of houses, repairs, agricultural activities, and events like marriage and death, among others. *Busti Lobus* function in agricultural procedures. The character and timing of the work required is planned well beforehand, as different fields are ready for distinct functions, like sowing, weeding and harvesting, at different times of the year. Often, brisk action is needed for the process and a nuclear family alone is not sufficient to complete the task.

The millet, maize and dry rice crops are planted on the steep hillsides, far above the location of the *busti*. Those who own adjoining fields mostly plant them in the same year. Fields are roughly separated by stones, but work in these fields is conducted as if the separate fields were one big farming area. The people working on the fields do not receive any monetary return but are served snacks and refreshments during the day. Although only adults constitute *Lobu* groups, children are asked to help in functions like seed-sowing for millet and dry paddy. Cardamom being a cash crop does not necessitate *Lobu* help, and Nepali labour is commonly engaged during the harvesting of cardamom, and paid in cash; or the labour is paid half or a part of the produce.

It is important to point out that with abundant cardamom plantation in the region and substantial monetary returns, the need of *Lobu* assistance has reduced significantly. There is also a growing trend in the more affluent families to send hired help to represent their families instead of one of the family members. However, the need of representation remains fairly significant in spite of the emerging economic disparity among the Lepchas of Dzongu.

In case *Lobu* cannot be reciprocated because of some reason, for instance during busy seasons like the harvest time, then another kind of give-and-take activity takes places called the *Lobu-afar*, which is paid in terms of the produce obtained from the harvest. Returning help with money is called *lho*.

Lobus are also invited for cooking, making *chi* and serving food to guests during marriages and other functions of social importance. All families of a *Lobu* group are required to give a gift worth Rs. 500 to 1,000, two scarves and 10 or more bottles of liquor.[18] In case of death, one member of a family from each *Lobu* group accompanies the funeral procession and offers help in procuring wood for cremation. Assistance in death ceremonies is called *lhenthop*. Help extended in *lhenthop* is between Rs. 50 and 300 and is termed as *thamuyeth*. Traditionally, *thamuyeth* was also given in the form of 1 to 2 *pathi* millet (I *pathi* = 2 kg), 1 *pathi* maize and a bottle of *chi*. Today, however, *thamuyeth* mainly constitutes monetary help, and in case money is not available, then rice and vegetables may be offered as a substitute. Furthermore, the exchange of *chi* is no longer prominent at the instance of death, but *chi* and cloth for prayer flags are given on the 49th day after a person's death, when the entire *busti* is invited for a feast by the family of the dead. The practice of placing one rupee in the hands of the bereaved person by relatives and friends who attend the funeral is also not observed any longer.

Thamuyeth (condolence and payment) is in addition to *lhenthop*. The amount of *lhenthop* is proportional to the closeness of the concerned family or friendship. The *Lobu* relationship is somewhat asymmetric to the autonomous nuclear family of the Lepchas. Despite the fact that family property is a private sphere, the production from it acquires a fundamental collective dimension involving support from *Lobu* groups.

Lyangcho

Each family is involved in larger mutual help groups called *Lyangcho* (*busti* people) with whom one shares obligations and compulsions of perfunctory exchange. High involvement is observed in the social network of the Lepchas and virtually everyone is invited to social events like marriages and funerals. A bundle of wood for the funeral pyre is provided by the *busti* people and each family that attends the event brings gifts which are reciprocated. *Lyangcho* is also distinct from *Lobu* as it does not extend labour on an exchange basis. If someone needs additional labour, over and above what is provided by the *Lobu* group, then it can be done by hiring people from the *busti* willing to work for money, food, or grain. The practice of *Lyangcho* is not extremely common in Dzongu today, nevertheless, it does exist.

Ochhom

Apart from the *Lobu* and *Lyangcho* groups, a person's friends also form a co-operative enterprise. These friends could come from within or outside of the *busti*, or from one's own or any other *putso*. Mutual friendship is the only basis for this co-operative grouping and includes the offer of help and material objects and services, apart from a good measure of psychological support. A person could get labour, cattle and fields, among other things, on loan from his *ochhom*. This help group is distinct from other co-operative groups as no grave reciprocal obligations are prerequisites of this exchange. The practice of *ochhom* has seen a considerable decline in Dzongu today.

Ohlok

Each family of the *busti* also contributes to the *busti*'s public enterprises and welfare institutions. This collective group works for community welfare like the upkeep of paths, construction of bridges, monasteries, etc. and is organised by the local Panchayat. *Lobu*s are mobilised from the *busti* and a member of each household contributes towards the common cause. Those found missing from *ohlok* without a valid excuse may be fined Rs. 50 and a few bottles of *chi*. However, the fine is seldom exercised. A paid labourer is allowed to replace a male member in *ohlok*. The collaborative work-group culture carves through the boundaries of different neighbourhoods and age differences as a wide range of age groups participate in the common activities.

Every family in the *busti* is also required to support the village monastery or *gompa*. All *gompa*-sponsored errands are voluntary in nature, and the bi-monthly feasts held in the monastery are supported by the people of the *bustis* as well. Contributions and chores are compulsory and are given out to families on a rotation basis. A symbolic expression of the *busti* unity is also part and parcel of the religious life of these people. This can be illustrated by the Boom-Kor ceremony.[19]

CONFLICT RESOLUTION

The Lyang-Ganbu (village elders), along with other educated and respected members of the society, act as an ad hoc body where they try to resolve issues that have become a matter of dispute and have not been solved by either families or their *putsos*. These men discuss the problem at hand and try to arrive at a solution. If the outcome is not acceptable to both the parties concerned, then the matter is taken to the Panchayat. But this happens only on rare occasions.

Cases of crime are found to be rare, and strong disagreements are socially disapproved; theft among the Lepchas is highly unusual and, in fact, was known to be virtually non-existent. Theft is considered an unnatural phenomenon. The Lepcha canon is based on the principle that one does not need to steal to live, consequently, no precautions were taken against theft and no rituals or ceremonies conducted towards its avoidance.

The property of an individual is considered solely his domain and even picking fruit from the neighbour's tree is considered a wrongdoing. If a child commits a misdeed, he is admonished and given a thrashing. However, if a serious crime or theft did take place, the household in question would, traditionally, report the theft to the Mandal who would approach the suspected offender along with the Youmi and convince him to restore the stolen property. If he refused to comply, even though the evidence was against him, the matter was reported to court.

Today, Kyoung Shezum or *Samaj* members act as an informal council who help clear disputes and matters pertaining to crime. If these young representatives cannot solve a matter, the Panchayat has to be brought in to resolve disputes and criminal incidents.

Petty thefts like the picking of umbrellas, slippers and raincoats, however, are on the rise. I was also informed that some Nepali labourers have been caught trying to steal the riches entombed in *chotyens*. Nevertheless, even today people seldom lock their houses in remote Dzongu and, in my observation, theft, by and large, continues to be an alien aspect for the Rongs.

Lepchas are basically god-fearing people who are conscientious about paying taxes and are found to do so even if it means selling their crops or mortgaging land. Perhaps, the fear of land being confiscated, as could be the case during the monarchy, still lingers in their minds. Lepchas are a calm populace who try to avoid disputes of all kinds.

The Gompa Society takes care of all the religious transgressions. The Gompa is responsible for the bi-monthly rituals and these ceremonies are sponsored in rotation by two families. Offences of sorcery by the Lama and Mun are also known to occur on occasions and are solved by the Gompa Society as well. A solemn oath along with a religious ceremony is usually sufficient to relieve the offender if he denies the charge. Perjury is considered the most serious crime for the Lepchas and the guilty and his family are publicly rejected and excluded from all social events of the *busti*. A perjurer among one's ancestors constitutes a hereditary stain. It is believed that if one commits perjury, his descendants will die young. A history of perjury in a family is also taken into account while arranging marriages. Every effort is made to cut out rows after feasts. The Lamas even invoke and destroy Addhit Mung, the demon of quarrels, before the initiation of any public or private ceremony.

An elaborate ritual used to be held in the monastery annually, during autumn, to destroy the enmity of speech, thought and action. But if a row did break out, a mutual friend of the two has to host a feast and try to mediate between the two and come to a solution. If the quarrel prevailed without an obvious reason, it was considered the action of malicious spirits and then exorcism—the ultimate resort—was tried. This annual ritual is not performed any longer in Dzongu.

In case of a serious dispute, the Lepchas try to resolve the problem from within, as approaching the Mangan court is taken as a slur on the community. In such circumstances, the Panchayat is taken into confidence and the Panchayat members visit the quarrelling parties and try to understand the intricacies of the dispute and find a solution.

Traditionally, however, this role was played by the Gyapon who would employ his tact to soften the stands of the parties and find a resolution. If this failed, he would command the parties to prepare *chi* and keep an exorbitant sum of money ready. The *chi* takes about eight to nine days to prepare during which time the Gyapon and village elders try repeatedly to mollify the disputing groups. If this does not work, then the Gyapon would warn them of taking the matter to the Mandal who would fine the two groups a large sum of money. The Gypon would then sneakily name an exorbitant amount of fine that he thought the Mandal might inflict on the troublemakers. This would clearly be out of reach for the people concerned. Thus, the offenders would be suitably stunned, and plead for a reduction and try to patch up the dispute. The Gyapon and Youmi would then settle for a smaller fine from which all of them would, of course, eat and drink together, and the Gyapon would advocate the virtues of being amiable. At the end, the fine was returned and order restored. Today, however, it is the Panchayat and the village elders who resolve disputes in consultation with the educated members of the society.

It may be said that that the Lepchas continue to retain much of their socio-political and communal traditions without much interference from the outside world. The base-structure retains its self-styled autonomy and the control is maintained by the village elders, Panchayat and the Kyoung Shezum.

DECISION-MAKING

The ultimate right of decision making in a family lies with the head of the family or the eldest male member. Today, the opinion of the educated members of a family is also given due consideration. Decisions are also taken in consultation with the senior female members of a family and spouses along with other members of the family. In matters pertaining to larger social groups, informal assemblies of educated members of the *bust*, the Panchayat and village elders often decide for the larger community. In cases where a conflict cannot be resolved by the informal group, the matter is carried forward to the Panchayat who consult the educated people in the *busti* and arrive at a resolution.

RELIGION

In Geoffrey Gorer's *The Lepchas of Sikkim* (1937), he notes that,

> the discussion on the Lepchas' religion is rendered extremely difficult by the fact that they practice simultaneously, and without any feeling of theoretical discomfort, two (or probably three) mutually contradictory religions.[20]

The religious practices of the Lepchas of Dzongu may be classified into three categories:

- Lamaism
- The Mun religion
- The worship of their ancestors, or the 'People of Mayel'

As Gorer rightly pointed out, it is important to note that it becomes problematic to treat these three divisions as three distinct impermeable aspects of their faith. Although the three facets might represent the different stages in the Lepcha's religious history, they are not necessarily evolutionary in nature and are found to be in practice today in an intricate synthesis. The adoption of Lamaism by the Lepchas was perhaps not necessarily dramatic as there are indeed some striking similarities between Lamaism and the Mun religious practices. To begin with, in both the schools of faith, the gods and spirits can be munificent, malicious or neutral; and not unlike the Hindu gods, the same gods and spirits could be benign when content and malevolent if angered. Rituals were given great importance and were aplenty, and though the cause and interpretation of dreams differed, they were considered meaningful and prophetic in both the religions.

The Lepchas are believed to have readily adopted Lamaism but not its individualistic ethics as their ethos is based on social and communal lines. Gorer writes that the Lepchas also did not give much impetus to the idea of reincarnation based on personal deeds as their fate was decided by the horoscope and the time of birth and death. The idea of sin in Lamaism also did not find easy acceptance among the Lepchas. It is reported that the word for sin used by the Lepchas, *layo*, is borrowed from Tibetan. Gorer noted that the only act which they considered sinful was the killing of animals. Except a few who had accepted Lamaism, others did not actually use the term *layo* but *nam-toak*, which roughly translates to 'actions not approved by the supernatural beings'. Some such actions did not even affect the evil-doer.[21] However, here it must be mentioned that today the Lepcha consciousness has perhaps undergone a metamorphosis and apart from perjury, which was indeed considered a heinous sin, the influence of the world outside, not to mention the deluge of Hindu mainstream morality via the glitzy family dramas on Star Plus (a big favourite of the unsuspecting folks here), has induced a growing sense of sin and morality that, reading from the earlier accounts on the Lepchas, was perhaps absent from their daily demeanour.

It would not be incorrect to state that today Lamaism seems to be finding favour with the Lepchas of Dzongu. The headmaster of the Lingthem School, in upper Dzongu, even referred to the Mun religion as 'their past'. The reason for this shift is perhaps owing to the organised and institutional nature of Lamaism as compared with their indigenous religion. The Head Lama of Tholung Gompa, Chedup Lepcha, gets a salary of Rs. 2,000 from the government every month, but no such benefits come to the Lepcha priests. The prominence of Lamaism in the region is not least because the Lepchas do not consider Lamas as dramatically different from their own priests. Also, not only are their own priests fast dwindling but their power is believed to be diminishing as well. This is so because with the Lama influence, the Lepchas started to cremate their dead and not bury them as was their earlier practice. They now claim that cremating their priests results in the decrease in their powers, as a result the reincarnated spirit is less powerful. Lepchas also find it more prestigious to be identified with 'Buddhism'. This attitude prevailed as Lamaism was the religion of the Bhutias (Tibetans who migrated to Sikkim) who comprised Sikkim's monarchy before it's amalgam with the Indian union. The influence of the religion of the ruling class was substantial as is reported by scholars and Lepchas alike, so much so that some of the Lepchas who were appointed Kazis (high ranking officers) readily abandoned their Lepcha practices for the new ones and even married Bhutia women, thereby making the transformation a smooth one. Even so, it is reported that the Lingthem Monastery's head Lama's corrupt image during the 60s and 70s resulted in only a few Lamas following the vocation. Albeit, since the 90s there has been a steady increase in the same.

Lamaism

The form of Buddhism practised in Sikkim is termed as Lamaism and not Buddhism by most scholars, as the faith practised in

Sikkim stems from Mahayana Buddhism of the Nyingmapa Sect and not Hinayana or Vajrayana. This means that their connection with Buddhism is via the Mahayana Buddhist texts. Also the adaptation, exemplified by practices like animal sacrifice (even within the monastery grounds), requires qualification.

Gorer describes the key traits of Lamaism as thus:

> Priesthood and sanctity are acquired by learning and not by inspiration; the sacrifice of animals is a heinous sin; the future can be learned by calculations from the holy books and not by inspiration; the soul of the dead wanders for a short time in a sort of purgatory, before being reincarnated either in another form on this earth, or going to some heaven or hell, as different as imagination can make them from anything experienced on earth. Most important of all, Lamaism ethics are founded on a belief in individual destiny and a sense of sin, Lamaism contains a long, explicit and detailed list of sins which can be performed by human beings, and which are visited on the evil-doer, first by feelings of remorse and secondly by punishment either in this life or in future reincarnations.[22]

The majority of the people of Dzongu are Buddhist barring a small population of Christians that are, barring a few exceptions, mainly centred in Lower Dzongu—in the *busti*es of Lum, Gor, Sangtok and Shyagyong. But so far, there are no churches within the limits of Dzongu and the Christians conduct their service in groups in people's homes. They also visit the church in Mangan on occasions. It is reported that the Christian community made an attempt to construct a church about five years ago around 1998 but this was stopped as the majority feared it would result in the further spread of Christianity in the region. Christianity finds little favour with the Buddhists of Dzongu as they believe that adopting the Christian faith not only signifies abandoning Buddhism but also their indigenous religion, as unlike Lamaism, Christianity has to be practised in isolation and cannot be combined with other belief systems. Locals claim that a reason for adopting

Christianity is perhaps because of its low cost, as both Lamaism and the Mun religion are highly ritualistic in nature. As stated by the only doctor posted in Dzongu, Dr. Gyamtso Bhutia, who recently lost his mother, "conducting our rituals is an extremely expensive affair, and if there is a death in the family we even go into debt and it takes a long time to financially recover from the event."

The origin of Lamaism in Sikkim can be traced back to the coronation of the first Maharaja of Sikkim in 1642. Tapan Chattopadhyay writes:

> When Lhatsun Chhembo and his belligerent associates set foot on this land (Sikkim), the land was already ripe for capture. The clever Chhembo did not make any mistake in assessing the situation. He installed a dynasty blessing it with his family title of 'Namgyal' and got himself a place in history as the 'patron saint of Sikkim'. Moreover, in an elaborate ceremony, he worshipped the Lepcha god Kongchen-Konghlo with so much devotion that it did not fail to impress the aborigines. The British missionaries showed a like wisdom years later, when they worshipped Goddess Kali in Calcutta praying for their success in spreading Christianity.[23]

A.R. Foning in his book *Lepcha: My Vanishing Tribe* notes:

> The setup of our society is such that ranking and gradation is completely out of place; and it could be said with emphasis that there never has been any acknowledgement of authority save those of the seniors in our tribe. It can be asserted with equal emphasis that we Lepchas never had any king amongst us. Whatever kings we had and know of, were the Namgyal kings of the later evolved country of Renjyong or Sikkim carved out within our 'sanctum sanctorum', nay Mayel Lyang. The ancestors of these kings were installed in 1642 at Yoksam with our consent. This too was done because a few generations earlier, patriarch Tekung Tek, who was a Bonthing (priest of the indigenous religion of the Lepchas) but never a chief, as has been made out, was coaxed into ceremoniously swearing eternal friendship of brotherhood with the Tibetans who were gradually infiltering into our land.

The person responsible for this vital task was Khye-Bumsa, the far-sighted and brilliant ancestor of the later kings. Eventually, as a result of this friendship pact, we agreed innocently to accept kings among us and we as a tribe have upheld them ever since.[24]

Chattopadhyay adds:

Legends also tell that Tibetans destroyed Rongs' scriptures which were the preserves of a few and obliterated their alphabets in a bid to facilitate propagation of Lamaism. In the process, they freely extended their religious frontiers and trespassed into Rong mythology. It was done so smoothly that it is difficult today to formally demarcate the area of the trespass. The Rong psyche made this possible for them. The same psyche made possible a symbolic relationship between Muns and Lamas, rums and moongs, Guru Rimpoche and the Buddha in their religious system without an iota of discomfort. In fact, their strange beliefs will not be correctly understood except in the background of this symbiosis.[25]

The Lepchas of Sikkim, and certainly those of Dzongu, wholeheartedly agree with the above observation while the Bhutias vehemently oppose it. But, emotions and political mileage aside, in consequence of the lack of concrete proof, as is clearly stated in the above passage, it is important to study Chattopadhyay's critique with the utmost discretion till further study is conducted in the area, and the idea either abandoned or endorsed.

The form of Lamaism practised in the state originates mainly from the Mahayana school of Buddhism combined with Tantric Hinduism, some Chinese and Mongolian elements and the Tibetan Bon religion—pre-Buddhist faith of Tibet. This branch of Buddhism has often been considered inferior and referred to as mere 'priestcraft' by scholars. Also, this branch of Lamaism has been considered as "un-Buddhistic" by L.A. Wadell (1934).

Chattopadhyay in *Lepchas and their Heritage* outlines the journey of Lamaism into Sikkim:

Lamaism is essentially priestcraft and an impure form of Buddhism that was introduced in Tibet in the middle of the seventh century. It owed it's origin to tantrism supposed to have been propagated by Arya Asanga, a Buddhist monk of Peshawar, who lived about 300 AD.... It (Buddhism) was the earliest organised religion with the quickest spread (later, Christianity and Mohammedanism have dimmed its record) and four great councils were held in different areas and climes to regulate its missionary growth... the fourth council at Jalandhar in the Punjab held under the aegis of King Kanishka (1st century AD) of Kashmir and the Punjab witnessed a schism over the polemic of exorcism between the 'northern' and the 'southern' schools which led to the evolution of the Mahayana Buddhism. While the 'southern school' advocated the more primitive and purer form with Pali as the medium, the 'northern school' incorporated bolder concepts of a progression of several grades of theoretical Buddhas and of numerous divine Budhisatwas... When 'northern' Buddhism found its way to Tibet through the good offices of Sron-tsan Gampo's Chinese wife, it had already gathered dregs of impurity... Nevertheless, tantrism was not so much of a force then in Tibet than a hundred years later, when Padmasambhava came to this country at the request of King Khri-Sron-De-Tsan (755–797 AD). He introduced tantric Buddhism in Tibet which held a steady sway for about 300 years, though it broke into many sects and developed signs of morbidity and decadence. It was at this critical juncture that in 1042 AD that Chandragarbha @ Atish (982–1054) visited Tibet from Vikramashila Buddhist University in Bihar... (Chandragarbha) had traveled far and wide including Sumatra and risen then to fame as the brightest luminary of the Buddhist lore, was no believer in magic but preached celibacy, moral abstinence and shunning of the practice of magic... He took a synthetic view of the 'Mahayana' and 'Hinayana' traditions of Buddhism and established monastic discipline among Tibetans, bringing the majority of them under its influence. The reformed sect was called the Kah-dam-pa or 'those bound by orders'. Three and a half centuries later, in another reformer Tsong-kha-pa's hands the order became more ritualistic and less ascetic and became known as Ge-lugs-pa or 'Yello Hats'—the most dominant sect in Tibet... Incidentally, Ge-lugs-pa later found favour with Mangolian rulers and their protagonist Bsod-nams-rgya-mtsø (1546–1587) came to be recognised by the ruler Altan Khan of Thumed Mongolia as the first veritable Dalai ("Ocean').

> The conferment of sovereignty of the whole of Tibet on the fifth Dalai Lama (1615–1680) by the Mongolian chief Gusri Khan was only a predictable follow-up. Those who continued to subscribe to the old tantric beliefs and mode of dressing and refused to be reformed came to be known as Rnin-ma-pa; or 'Red Hats'. Lhatsun Chhembo and his two companions imported into Sikkim this latter variety of Buddhism in which Guru Rimpoche seems to occupy a more important place than even the Buddha himself.
>
> There was yet another variety—Kar-ma-pa, an offshoot of the Kargyupa sect founded by Atisha's friend and pupil Lama Marpa in the second half of the eleventh century that found its way into Sikkim. Marpa himself was married but Kargyupas meditated in caves and practiced mahamudras as the mode of obtaining spiritual insight. Kar-ma-pas, on the contrary, imbibed certain aspects of the Rnin-ma-pa worship, believing in 'hidden revelations on the tantric cult and were hardly celibate.
>
> ...as soon as the news of his (Buddha's) death (May, 544 BC) spread, a section of monks like Subhadra became jubilant and thought that this was the end of the tyranny of the monastic order... Within a hundred years, the Master's final foreboding came true and dissension arose among with regard to his actual words and their interpretations. In a couple of hundred years, eighteen or more sects came into existence. But all his intellectual power would have found it difficult to conceive a phenomenon like the Lama of the Tibetan or the Sikkimese variety, who is content to look at the world through his inscrutable laden eyes, having drugs or sex on the sly and turn the meditative time-wheel with monotonous precision. The absence of contemplative or intellectual element in practical Lamaism is dangerous, because this will eventually make all rituals, arts, moral legislation and the 'active life' in general fall apart through lack of principle to unify them. Today in Sikkim a Lama is made, not born, and priestcraft is learnt and sanctity acquired by constant practice and not by inspiration. At least this dictum applies to the ordinary Lamahood, while the higher posts may need vicarious traits and considerations, sometimes looking beyond regional boundaries.[26]

The 28-year-old Lama Yeshay Lepcha, a Lama since the past twenty years and presently a teacher at the Lingzya Sheda established in 1997, admitted that Lamahood attracts few aspirants. He also mentioned the existing dichotomy in the lifestyle of the Lamas. Talking of his impending marriage, he smiled and confessed that "Lamas acknowledge that marriage distracts one away from reaching enlightenment but most Lamas marry. Also, in the recent years they have started to propagate vegetarianism but most Lamas consume flesh without an iota of discomfort." Talking of the onerous job of adopting Lamahood, he said that there was the need to maintain a pious exterior for the benefit of the masses. He further divulged that he went to the cinema in civilian clothes.

Over the years, the philosophy and practices of Lamaism have combined in a big way with the indigenous faith of the Lepchas—referred by some as the Mun faith. The fusion is so complete that it is now difficult to decipher with certainty the origin of the prevalent religious practices. The situation is further complicated as the Lamaistic teachings introduced in Sikkim were the unreformed Nying-Ma-Fa, the old sect which amalgamated many customs originating from the Bon in its religious practices. Among the Lepchas, Lamaism and the Mun religion are intermingled to such an extent that many Lepcha rituals are jointly performed by Mun priests as well as the Lamas. Gorer writes that even in mythology, the patron saint of the Lamas, Tasheything (Guru Rimpoche), was equated to Tak-bo-thing—an important Mun supernatural. Tasheything was also considered the husband of the Mun. It was on this alleged reason that the Lama deity was considered stronger than the Mun. This is a shift from the matriarchal beginnings of the Lepchas and their existing belief in which they continue to hold that the female supernaturals are more powerful than their male counterparts.

The horoscope cast on the third day after the birth of a child determined whether a child would become a Lama or not. The eldest sons of all the Lamas also automatically become Lamas (although there is an expectation from all the sons of

Lamas to acquire Lamahood). Hence, the horoscope was mainly used for laymen's sons. Incarnations of late Lamas are also encouraged to adopt the Lama practice. But in reality, these rules need not be practised as few are keen to commit their days to the task of learning religious books by heart. As a result, a majority of the children found in the *sheda* (monastic school), come from poor families, or in some cases are the offspring of Lamas. Gorer writes that the children chosen for Lamahood are traditionally presented with a yellow sash and taken to the monastic ceremonies for the purpose of familiarising the Lamas with their practices. However, as reported by the Lamas, the situation has changed today and the child is sent straight to the monastic school and receives his education along with other Lamas. A teacher was chosen for the budding Lama when he was at the age of about 10 to 15 years but one's own biological father could never be the teacher. The selected teacher had to be presented with a pig, *chi*, ceremonial scarf and a rupee. The child lived with the teacher for three years during which period he served him during the day and received instructions in the evening. The child was allowed to visit his home from time to time. The child was taught to read in the beginning and on occasions was taught to say prayers and play instruments. The first degree a Lama receives is called Chabri-bu. This is followed by six more grades which a Lama can receive. The following are the seven grades of Lamas in order of hierarchy.

1. Dorje Lapoon
2. Omzet.
3. Chitem-bu
4. Chene
5. Kane
6. Tongpemu-bu
7. Chabri-bu

The duties and privileges of each office are laid down in the tradition. But the Lamas had three main duties: personal devotions, monthly and calendarical services and ministering to the ill. It is also observed that the Lamaist ceremonies required less expenditure as compared with that of Mun religion. But if a Lepcha erected an altar in his house containing sacred scriptures, they would need to be taken out at least four times every year and read by the Lamas. Thus, the added expense of hiring, feeding and paying the Lamas would total to a substantial amount. This practice too has undergone a change as today it suffices to take out the scriptures only once a year.

Educated and responsible members of Dzongu like Y.T. Lepcha and Athup Lepcha, to name a few, are known to have rebelled against the Lamas though not against Lamaism. These individuals are responsible for various reforms in the Lama practice, including the misuse of monastery funds, decrease in the cost involved in the rituals and the barring of animal sacrifice in some of the monasteries. The practice of animal sacrifice was eventually stopped in the Lingthem monastery around 1977, while Lama Yeshay Lepcha reports that the Ship Gyer Gompa banned the practice only around 1995. The head Lama of the Tholung monastery Chedup Lepcha said animal sacrifice continues even today in the holiest monastery of Dzongu. Lepchas at large are unhappy about the teaching of Lamaism in Tibetan language and script. This points to a growing consciousness of the Lepcha identity as apart from other Lamaists in the state.

4

The Mun Religion

THE MUN RELIGION, FUNCTION AND RITUALS

The main function of the religion of the Lepchas of Dzongu or the Mun religion is to help people cope with suffering and seek relief. It is a means of achieving productivity and prosperity. The Lepchas were shamanists and powers both good and evil formed the basis of their religious system. All bad was the work of either evil or enraged benign spirits, to be exorcised or propitiated as the situation deemed fit. What could not be explained rationally was believed to be the action of the supernatural, and people's viability to cope with such acts formed the basis of the religious system. The Mun religion does not endorse the quest for personal salvation nor does it recognise individualism. It also does not have any social organisation. Nonetheless, the purpose of the religion is not purely utilitarian as there exist beliefs and practices that cannot be explained purely in terms of their needs. The Lepchas have numerous gods and goddesses who they worshipped regularly. However, it is observed that this was done more to evade misfortune and the wrath of the gods than any sublime spiritual quest.

The Mun religion outlines the presence of eight souls, *a-pil*, in man and six in women. After a person dies, one *a-pil* goes to the skies in search of Rum-Lyan or paradise while the remaining go to the bosom of the Mother Earth. The Lepchas believe that there exist good spirits or Rum and evil spirits or Mung. Even so, a good spirit may, at times, cause harm when angered. Forests, mountains, rivers, rocks and other natural objects are believed to be the dwelling places of the spirits. All catastrophes (poor harvests, hailstorms, illness, etc.) are said to be caused by spirits and thus need to be propitiated along with the mandatory sacrifice and rituals.

Rituals are woven around securing a long and healthy life with few misfortunes and release from illness and natural disasters. The Lepchas perform curing and purification rights as well. The element of the supernatural and man's responsibility to it are predominant, and rituals are believed to engender a harmonious relationship between man and the supernatural. Rituals generate a given worldview, reinforce the importance of institutional structures and work to strengthen social relationships. Rituals are also important social events and serve as a meeting ground for the people who gather in large numbers to eat, drink and socialise on religious occasions. Rites and rituals also help restore peace and normalcy in difficult situations.

The economic cost of the religious ceremonies is mainly borne by the locals. The participation in religious activities is deemed important and absence from rituals can bring about action against the absentee from the religious heads (though in reality this seldom happens). Rituals often involve animal sacrifice and can be an expensive affair. Nonetheless, the Lepchas are known to often give precedence to religious activities and even come into debt to provide for religious feasts. Ordinary people cannot deal with the spirits directly and hence require the expertise of the local practitioners or Muns and Bongthings.

DIFFERENCES BETWEEN LAMAS AND THE LEPCHA PRIESTS (MUNS AND BONGTHINGS)

Let us look at the main differences between Lamaism and the Mun religion:

Unlike Lamaism, the Mun religion does not have any social organisation. The Lepcha religious priests are people who, owing to the possession by a supernatural, have certain gifts and duties. But their status is not enhanced by any title. The 61-year-old Mun, Sungkun Lepcha of Lingdong says, "My mission is to conduct the various ceremonies and rituals required of me by the people. Like people work in fields I do pooja." Bongthing Kenchoy Lepcha of Pentong says,

> The spirit was supposed to come in me so it did. Fate. That's all. I'm fine with it. It's my duty and if I do not obey it and abandon my calling then all misfortunes will fall on me. I am scared of that prospect.

The Muns and Bongthings also do not have any special dress distinguishing them from the average Lepcha. Also, unlike Lamaism, it is not considered happy to be a Mun who has to sacrifice many animals in the course of his practice. This aspect of a Mun too is accepted as an act of fate and complied to. What's more, no special ceremony takes place when a Mun dies, as the spirit that had possessed the Mun is believed to have no concern with the soul of the dead. Another important disparity between the two religions is the status of their female priests. Female Lamas or *in-e-bu* are subordinate to Lamas and are not allowed to conduct ceremonies or perform exorcism on par with female Muns. In the Rong pantheon, however, women occupy a more important place than men, hence in the Mun religion the female Muns are considered not just equals but superior to their male counterparts.

THE LEPCHA PRIESTS

The Mun and Padem/Bongthing are the main priests of the Lepchas and have been described by scholars as sorcerers. The

Mun and Bongthing are believed to possess the powers to avert and thwart the influence of harmful spirits and cure illness, among other things.

The Muns were also responsible for performing numerous ceremonies that are connected with the worship of good spirits and deities and the appeasement of demons. They performed all the rites dealing with the important events of the life of the Lepchas. Mun ceremonies are performed for both the individual, his household and for a geographical group of households (*putso* and *busti*). The presence of the Mun was mandatory during birth, death, purification rites, expelling devils, and marriage, among other ceremonies and occasions.

The Bongthing mediates between the members of the *Putso* and their guardian spirit or Rum. The services of the Bongthing were also required in all ceremonies that deal with Rum. He can also conduct other ceremonies with the exception of the rites that deliver the soul of the dead. This ceremony can only be performed by the Mun. Gorer outlines major functions of the Mun:

> To get rid of Sor moong (violent death) or Apang moog (genital-urinary diseases); to drive away the ghost of dead children by infantile diarrhea; and to get rid of Chyom moong (that is the devil who causes people to die by falling from a tree or chiff) or Rot moong (that is the devil who causes people to commit suicide.[27]

Men called Pau (also spelt as 'Pawo' by Veena Bhasin in *Ecology Culture and Change: Tribals of Sikkim Himalayas*), and women known as Nandjemu or Nyen-Jo-Mo are other important sorcerers that are believed to be possessed by Tibetan deities. Consequently, this interesting religion continues to practise many aspects of the Bon faith of pre-Buddhist Tibet and thus helps preserve it. Many rituals here are observed to be independent of the influence of Lamaism.

The powers of the Pau are mainly utilised in case of fire or for the prevention of fire accidents. The male Yaba and female

Yama are another group of Lepcha sorcerers of minor importance and are said to be possessed by Limbu spirits. The Yaba and Yama are mainly found in the Darjeeling district and are said to be absent in the areas east of the Tista and North Sikkim.[28] They conduct ceremonies that prevent accidental death caused by Arvath Moong. The *Mun-ha* are exorcisers and Pa-yok assists the Mun. Tung-li Mun and Mun-mook Mun correspond to the white and black magicians, respectively, of mainstream religions.

It is observed that Mun and Bongthing are considered priestess and priest, respectively, among the Lepchas. However, within Dzongu there is no clear demarcation of the sex of the Mun. Even the word Bongthing is said to have been rarely used in Dzongu till some decades back when the word Padem was more in use. This can be illustrated by the words of Gorer:

> Both men and women can be Mun, but only men can be Padem (or Bumthing as they are called outside Zongu); these are both pure Lepcha spirits and are essentially similar, save that the Padem are far less powerful, and that instruction by an already qualified Padem is optional, whereas for Mun, a three year course of instruction is obligatory. Padem are weaker than Mun and capable of exorcising far fewer devils; they cannot prophesy nor perform the death ceremony. For many men Padem is the first step to becoming Mun.[29]

The uncertainty pertaining to the sex of the Mun in Dzongu can be further illustrated by the fact that at present there are reportedly eight Muns in all of Dzongu, out of which only two are female while six are male. It is also difficult to say with certainty as to when the use of the word Bongthing became popular as compared with Padem. The 70-year-old Bongthing, Kenchyok Lepcha of Pentong, one of the most remote and cut-off *busties* of Dzongu, says that though the term 'Bongthing' is commonly used by Lepchas, people in his *busti* still address him as Padem. He also says that both the terms 'Bongthing' and 'Padem' were used even during his grandfather's time.

The number of other remaining Lepcha priests in Dzongu at present is as follows:

Bongthing – 16 (all male)
Nyen-Jo-Mo – 1 (Female, 78-year-old from Ship-Gyer)
Pau – 1 (Male, 21-year-old from Lingthem)
Tung-li Mun – 1 (Male, Namprik)[3]

MAKING OF THE MUN

The role of the Mun and Bongthing is inherited within the family or *putso* (clan), with a member of the family chosen by the supernatural powers who protect him and, at times, possess the individual as well. Although Munship is hereditary, it does not necessarily appear in every generation. Anyone can become a Mun provided they acquire the necessary supernatural powers. The process of picking a Mun is determined by symptoms of mental depression or illness. A person may also become a Mun by an intimate involvement with a powerful spirit, who by that acquisition alone can become a Mun. An experienced Mun or Mun-mo confirms whether the symptoms are the advent of Mun on the individual. Bongthing Kenchoy Lepcha claims that he was possessed by the spirit when he was 45-year-old. He says that like everything else, his possession was fated, "When I was 30 years old, a Mun during my grandfather's time told me that a spirit would come to me and that I should honour it." He adds,

> I believe that the spirit in me is my grandfather's who was also a Mun. I know that from the things I am told I said when I was first possessed. Also, the method in which I conduct the rituals is the same as my grandfather's. If I try another way then the spirit does not come to me.

He described the experience of being possessed as an extremely powerful one,

> When the spirit first came to me my heart started beating fast. I became delirious and had the feeling of being in a dream-like state. It was a powerful experience and there was little scope of feeling scared.

Kenchoy was married at that time and said that his wife too accepted the situation without a problem. After the attainment of Munship, there is no restriction on the Mun's sexual activity, marriage, etc.; neither is there any requisite criterion of age for Munship.

From past accounts it is clear that the Mun underwent a rigorous training for a period of three years.[30] The practice of a training period for the Mun is also mentioned by Gorer but he does not state the period of training. According to him, the training under a senior Mun of the same or different sex would begin until the understudy received the *loong* or ceremonial qualification. However, this too has undergone a change and the Muns no longer go through any special training. Today, the method of training a Mun is much the same as that of other priests who pick up the necessary knowledge by observing the older priests. 67-year-old Mun Sungkun Lepcha, of Lingdong, could not even recollect clearly that such a practice existed. He says, "I have heard that Muns underwent training. But that time has gone. The knowledge I have gathered was acquired by watching my grandfather and my uncle who were both Muns."

GODS AND GODDESSES

The spirits Itpomu and Narzong-nyou are considered the most important spirits of the Mun. Narzong-nyou is the most important supernatural, and, besides Kanchenjunga, she is the presiding deity of Renzong (Sikkim) as well. Narzong-nyou is responsible for the geography, flora and fauna of the Lepchas. Her husband Komsithing was considered important but was not worshipped as he was considered a foreigner. The two are believed to have engendered a number of institutions and habits prevelant in the Rong society. Itpomu is not directly invoked but her creativity is eulogised. The supernaturals Mit Rum and De Rum are other important deities who are said to be ancestral gods and look after the dead Lepchas. The deity Tak-bo-thing also acquired considerable importance (equated with Tasheything or Guru Rimpoche).

REASONS FOR EXTINCTION

It is interesting to note that with the death of Muns, their spirit seems to be dying as well. The spirit does not find another body and their reincarnation is becoming rarer by the day. In fact, observing from thc past and prevalent trends, it is perhaps not out of line to state that it is only a matter of time before the Lepcha priests disappear completely even from their 'last resort' the Lepcha reserve of Dzongu. Also, not only are their own priests fast dwindling but their power is believed to be diminishing as well. This is so because with the Lama influence, the Lepchas started to cremate their dead and not bury them as was their earlier practice. They claim that cremating their priests results in the decrease in their powers. As a result, the reincarnated spirit is less powerful. Also, their chief function of driving away evil spirits is of little value in a world of strict forest regulations and a lifestyle in which the Lepchas of Dzongu are certainly not isolated from the rest of the world. The Lepchas believe that some of the evil spirits have gone away or disappeared because of the changing scenario. Another reason cited is the clearing of forests in certain areas as the woods are traditionally believed to be the abode of both good and evil spirits.

Other reasons given are the changes that took place in the last few decades, such as: Access to modern medicine and doctors decreased the dependence on the Mun. The spread of education and greater awareness resulted in a growing number of people to question their traditional belief system and seek tangible explanations. This also resulted in the surfacing of the ill-impacts of consumption of large quantities of *chi* and other alcoholic drinks. In fact, alcohol started to be considered, by some, as a major reason for their backwardness. *Chi* was an essential ingredient in the rituals of the Lepcha priests and this growing awareness perhaps had an adverse impact on their further proliferation. Shift to settled agricultural practices and the farming of cardamom resulted in greater predictability of harvests which affected the Mun's existence as well.

As discussed in the earlier chapter, Lamaism is perhaps a reason as well for the dwindling of the Lepcha priests. Rip Roshina Gowloog notes in his book *Lingthem Revisited*:

> It appears that under the Buddhist regime of the Chogyals in Sikkim a strong pro-Lamaist, if not anti-Mun, discourse was prevailing there for fairly long time. This discourse was prevailing there for a very long time. This discourse was translated in various forms. One of the common instances of this was the legendary story about the test of supremacy between a Mun and a Lama from Tibet identified as Guru Rimpoche or Padmasambhava, in which the latter had emerged victorious. This story had spread among the Lepchas and Bhutias of Sikkim and Darjeeling for a very long time. As a matter of fact it is still alive. Another aspect of this discourse was the spread of the belief that the Muns or Bongthings of later years were not as powerful as their predecessors. They often told that that later Muns were of no use as their "power" had diminished.[31]

Gowloog adds that with growing monetisation after the 1950s

> domestic animals proved to be an important source of cash income instead of remaining mainly as objects of sacrifice. Making sacrifice was also a part of Lamaism, but this change in the value of the domesticated animals seems to have affected their traditional religious order more than the Lamaist one because sacrifice of animals occupied a central role in the former whereas it occupies only a peripheral position in Lamaism. One of the most important developments that boosted Lamaism in Sikkim and relegated the traditional order to further oblivion was the settling of the Dalai Lama in India since 1959. This has been acknowledged by many observers to be responsible for the rejuvenation of the Lamaist order, not only in Sikkim but in the whole of India (Ling 1991). The Lamas who were not very

> different from the Muns and Bongthings until then began to receive more respect and attention.[32]

STATUS AND CHANGE

The Mun do not have a social organisation. Priesthood is identified in an individual by the possession of a spirit said to be present in the family lines. Priesthood here carries no titles. Nevertheless, the Lepcha priests were regarded with awe and respect by the people as is stated by the author AR Foning: "Literature has been one of the powerful means which has given them a position more important than that of other members of the community."[33]

But, today, with the coming of the Lamas, their esteem in society has somewhat dwindled and so has the extent and influence of their functions. Bomthing Natok Lepcha is at present the only Bomthing in Lingthem, the most populous *busti* of Dzongu. Being the only priest in the village, he is in great demand and only gets about two days off in a month. He remembers the times when the quaint *busties* of Dzongu were abuzz with scores of Muns and Bongthings scurrying off to drive away the next troublemaking devil,

> When I was a boy there were about 15 priests in Lingthem and they were all equally busy. But today, with the lack of faith they have stopped appearing; and just as well. If they were here today we wouldn't have enough to eat.

He feels that the Mun religion has taken a setback to Lamaism and the advent of modern medicine. Talking of his younger days, he reminisced, "Earlier people would call us often, but now Mun is finished, Bomthing is finished, Yaba and Yama is finished," he exclaimed between sucking at the omnipresent 'bamboo' filled with the mildly inebriating *chi*.

Bongthing Kenchyok Lepcha of Pentong, one of the remotest and cut-off *busti*es of Dzongu, says,

> Earlier when I went to perform a ritual, the people would arrange the preliminary accourerments for the pooja, but now I have to

go and prepare everything myself. Young people these days are not interested.

Talking of the change in their status in society he said,

> I am glad to be from Pentong. In lower Dzongu and some other Busties the young people even ridicule us at times. Earlier, people gave us a lot of respect but it is not the same now.

He mentioned that the time taken in conducting rituals has reduced considerably as well,

> The pooja that would take one hour now takes 20 minutes. People do not have patience. The expenditure on the rituals has also reduced and so has the dedication of the priests.

He also mentioned the changes in the nature of sacrifice saying,

> Earlier the rituals to ward off disease were much more elaborate. An ox or pig would be sacrificed but now we have to propitiate the spirits with just the sacrifice of a chicken.

ANCESTOR WORSHIP

- Its description and distinction from the Mun religion
- Changes

Its description and distinction from the Mun religion

The Lepchas believe that they originated from the 'People of Mayel', who they consider as their ancestors. Legend has it that the People of Mayel live in an unknown location close to Kanchenjunga. They are the children of the Goddess Narzong-nyou. These seven brothers are the guardian-deities of crops. The worship of these (? mythical) people, and the belief in Pong Rum (the god of hunters) form another facet of their religious system.

This is described as distinct from the Mun religion by Gorer even though the rituals are conducted by Muns because of the following reasons:

> It seems to me possible that the worship of the people of Mayel, and perhaps of Pong Rum the god of hunters, is of a different

> origin to the other Mun ceremonies; unfortunately too little is known about the ritual of neighbouring tribes to enable profitable speculation to be made as to whether either or both are relatively modern importations from outside, or whether, they are on the contrary the oldest Lepcha customs. The most outstanding differences with other Mun ritual, and indeed with ordinary Lepcha life, is, first, a discrimination against women, secondly, an insistence on virginity for some of the celebrants, and thirdly a suggestion of the danger of menstruating women. Women may perform sacrifice to the people of Mayel, but if they do so the ceremony is curtailed and fewer objects employed; they not only cannot sacrifice to Pong Rum but must not even be aware when the sacrifice takes place; and the popped corn and chi which are employed in it, if not made by a man, which is preferable, must be made by a virgin girl. The chief offering to the people of Mayel are the lafet sacrifice and sakyou faat; the small bird for the lafet must be killed by a virgin boy, and the strained chi poured into the buttered cup by a virgin girl.[34]

This religious order is indeed distinct from the other aspects of their religion and, in fact, is rather uncharacteristic of the Rongs, as otherwise their women enjoy the same significance and rights as men, even in the sphere of their religion.

The worship of the People of Mayel is conducted during harvest and at the time of hunting. Legend has it that these seven brothers live in seven huts in the snow-bound environs of the Kanchenjunga. These people are said to be immortal and become children every morning, grow up during the day and become old towards the evening time. They are the gods of grain and the Lepchas pray to them for bountiful harvests and timely rain. The People of Mayel are said to be dressed in traditional Lepcha clothes woven from nettle fibre and bamboo hats and have huge goiters, a sign of prosperity and good harvests. Three brothers are the guardian-spirits who are known to keep vigil on the way to Mayel. These brothers are called Mayel Yookrum (also called Pong Rum) Mi-tik and Tomtik. The two eldest brothers are married to two sisters called Talyou-Nimu and Sangvo-Nimu. Their wives are worshipped as spirits of the earth as their bellies are taken to be cultivable lands on which seeds of rice, millet, and maize, sown by their husbands, are fertilised.

It is said that in the ancient times, the people of Mayal would come down and interact with the Lepchas. But this practice was discontinued perhaps because the people are not as pious as they used to be in the ancient times. Instead, the people of Mayel now send birds called Mayelfo to the Lepchas every year to remind them when to sow the seeds, and when to harvest. The ancestors were worshipped in connection with dry rice, millet, and maize, while crops like buckwheat, wheat, barley and wet rice were not related to the people of Mayel and for this reason no prominent ceremonies took place for these crops. Gorer says that the ancestors were worshipped both after sowing and harvesting the dry rice.[35] The ceremonies conducted for the People of Mayel have already been described in detail by Gorer.

The Lepchas living in Dzongu at present may not have gone to Mayel or even encountered any of their immortal ancestors but a strong attachment in their belief is clearly discernible among them even today.

Changes

It is reasonable to sum up that the Lepchas worshipped the People of Mayel and even feared them because of the belief that they could control the quantity and quality of their harvest. But today, with greater predictability and security in the same, most of the rituals associated with the People of Mayel too have perished. The importance of Pong Rum, the god of hunters, has taken a batting as well, as hunting has been banned by the forest authorities and relegated as a mere pass time for the Lepchas. Pong Rum is worshipped only rarely in Dzongu in the context of hunting, however, he is also worshipped on occasions when the Mun or Bongthing diagnose a person's chest pain as an attack of Pong Rum, and prescribe the sacrifice of a red rooster.

Dry rice was perhaps the most important crop associated with the worship of their ancestors. But, with the introduction of wet rice, the planting of dry rice has been more or less stopped. The importance of other crops associated with their ancestors, like maize and millet, has declined dramatically after the introduction of the highly lucrative cardamom in the region. But, it is of relevance to note that the people of Dzongu continue to remain rather attached to their ancestors and their lore. However, their relationship has undergone a transition from an essentially dependent one to an emotional and nostalgic bond that they cherish to this day.

Even today one can hear stories of people who were foolhardy enough to try the impossible and ventured to Mayel paying for this misadventure with their lives. 25-year-old Chuki Lepcha, the computer science teacher at the Lingthem School, held that she had heard of a monk from Bhutan who had tried to go to Mayel. She also mentioned a European mountaineer who is believed to have chanced upon two of their ancestors on his escapades in the Himalayas. While in Pentong I was also told that the People of Mayel have stored seeds of "all the crops" for the Lepchas and hidden them in a container of stone beyond the *busti* of Pentong for the day when all the crops of the world will die.

5

Festivals and Ceremonies

CEREMONIES FOR PROPITIATION OF SPIRITS

Cherim—This ceremony takes place twice every year in honour of the sacred mountain god of Khangchendzonga and also serves to appease evil spirits, protect crops from hailstorms, men from ill-health and marks the worship of nature. The lofty peak of Khangchendzonga occupies a very significant place in the age-old tradition of the Lepchas and features prominently in their religious life. The ceremony is performed by both, the Mun and Lama in which not only the Kanchenjunga, but all other prominent mountain peaks are worshipped as well. A festival followed by a feast used to be held in the monastery on the 15th of every month to pay homage to Khangchendzonga. This was sponsored by two households in turn. But this practice has changed; today, the feast is less elaborate and is funded by all the houses who contribute an equal amount of money towards the event. The practice was changed because some of the locals believed that maintaining the monthly feast proved to be a rather expensive venture for the Lepchas and, therefore, took measures to curtail it to humbler proportions. It is of relevance to note that with the limiting of the feast, the attendance for the ritual has shrunk considerably as well. This is perhaps because feasts are indeed fundamental to the social and religious life of the Lepchas. As we have seen, feasting and socialising have often more to do with the religious life of the Lepchas than the spiritual aspect of the ritual itself. Therefore, in the absence of feasting, the people perhaps see little reason in observing cultural or religious occasions and, in fact, in my observance, feel somewhat disconnected from the event. This ritual takes place around the month of March on the date prescribed in the Lepcha calendar, as is the practice for all other Lepcha festivals and ceremonies.

Madrum—The ceremony is performed on a hilltop to mollify the hunting goddess of Madrum. The Bongthing is accompanied by the male members of the household in question, to the hilltop for the ritual. The spot where the ritual is performed is flexible and can be conducted in any open space. A patch of earth is cleared of undergrowth, where four holes are dug in the ground with each holding a bamboo stick. A thatched roof of bamboo and leaves adorned with flowers is installed. Small quantities of rice, ginger, powder-rice, fish, duck, millet and *chebuk* (intoxicant) is given as offering. An odd number of lines are drawn, on which the offerings are placed and a lamp made of bamboo is lit. Throughout the ceremony, the Bongthing chants prayers and ritualistic couplets devoted to Madrum who is said to be responsible for fights, headaches, madness, drunk-fights and outbursts of temper. A hen and rooster are sacrificed on the occasion and offered to the goddess. The sacrificial hen and rooster are then cooked and duly consumed. The food is not to be touched or eaten by any female member. Unlike many of the below-mentioned ceremonies, the Lepchas of today perform this ceremony only rarely.

Mik Ka Ta Ba Mung—This ceremony is performed to appease the malicious Mik Ka Ta Ba Mung, who has one eye in the centre of the forehead, glides along the surface of waterbodies and is said to prowl around at night time. Lepchas are scared of the dark and believe that anyone who comes across this Mung will lose his life. It is said that even if his shadow falls on someone, he would fall ill. If some such incident takes place and if the person in question does not feel better in three days, then the help of a Mun or Bongthing is called upon and a goat is sacrificed to placate the spirit. The sacrifice and the ceremony are performed on the spot where the encounter with the Mung is believed to have taken place.

Luna Ji Mung—There are broadly two chief ceremonies performed to propitiate a very malignant spirit called Luna Ji Mung of the forest. A less elaborate ceremony is conducted once or twice a year with the offering of eggs, and a more extensive one is performed once in three years.

Lyang Rum—Lyang is another supernatural highly feared by the Lepchas. Twice every year, towards the end of the summer and during winter, a young black boar is sacrificed to appease this dangerous spirit. Lyang is invoked by the presiding Mun or Bongthing and requested to accept the sacrifice and spare the family for whom the ceremony is being performed.

Gye bo lung Ji Rum—The ceremony is conducted to propitiate the spirit Gye bo lung Ji Rum. This ceremony is conducted with the contribution of all the villagers and a pig is sacrificed on the occasion. Each male member gets a share of the meat proportional to his contribution of gifts, which he carries back home and shares with his family. The head of the pig is given to the Bongthing, while the tail to the individual who sacrifices the pig.

Padeem Rum Faat—This ceremony is performed by every Mun and Bongthing. The flowers of peach or *tak-po-bor* are important accessories for the ritual performed around March-April. It is said that Bongthings who do not conform to this tradition might stand to loose some of their powers.

Tandong Lho Rum Faat—Tandong is the name of a mountain in South Sikkim and a ceremony is performed for the deity of this peak. The entire *busti* gathers on an open clearing on a small hill where, led by the Bongthing, the *busti* dwellers prey to the bounty of mother nature. The remarkable thing about this ceremony is that it does not involve any animal sacrifice. The objects mandatory for this ritual are the *lofit*[36] and flowers.

This is followed by a merry feast for which all the *busti* members contribute equally and partake in the festivities.

Namaal—Namaal is the Lepcha New Year and is celebrated not only within the family and *busti*, but together with all the Lepchas of Dzongu. The celebrations are held at Namprik Dong—currently the social nucleus of Dzongu. The day marks the victory of the Lepchas over the much-dreaded Laso Moong (for details see Folklore), and thus a victory of good over evil. On this day, Namprik Dong assumes the atmosphere of a fairground and people congregate here to partake in an entire day of revelry with the performance of traditional Lepcha songs and dances. Ranks of stalls of clothes, food and drinks are installed for the celebrations. A Bongthing or Mun conducts a ceremony to mark the beginning of the New Year. A mock battle and the burning and throwing away of Laso Moong's effigy, amidst shouts of "*get away, get away you devil*," marks the high point of the day. The Bongthing then makes symbols of a mouse, snake, eagle, etc. out of millet and flour and then burns the symbols in the fire to signify the burning away of the past year's ill-luck (this custom is carried out by each household as well). People return to their homes and *busties* in the evening and continue the celebrations with the drinking of *chi* and alcohol. Namaal is held around the months of December-January.

CEREMONIES OF THE CLAN OR *PUTSO*[37]

Each p*utso* has its own particular deity and performs a ceremony in its honour. The ritual is conducted by a Bongthing and Mun for the male and female *putso* respectively. The ceremony includes preparation of *lofit*, amidst the chanting of prayers and involves the sacrifice of a rooster. Males usually have their origin in a mountain peak and the female *putso* in a lake or some water body. The female *putso* ceremony is performed for both male and female *putsos*. A ceremony is held every three years by the male members of a *putso* in the honour of their *putso*'s guardian spirit. Lopsang Lepcha of Upper

Lingthem, who belongs to the Athim Arm *putso,* is said to have originated from a lake called Sanklang Rum. The *putso* ceremony was conducted in his house after a gap of 18 years (the ceremony was last performed in his house when his parents were still alive, in 1985). The age-old practice was revived because Lopsang says, "In the last few months, my family suffered a reoccurring pattern of calamities like accidents, diseases, etc. I realised that it was because we had stopped performing the *putso* ceremony. So, after many years, we will again call upon our *putso* deity to protect us and sorrow and disease will leave this house." It is observed that the Lepchas today no longer feel the need to appease all the gods and spirits that were mollified by their ancestors. Ceremonies deemed mandatory by their parents no longer seem as sacrosanct. Even the practice of the *putso* ritual seems to have considerably lost ground among the Lepchas. Bongthing Natok Lepcha, arguably the busiest Lepcha priest in Dzongu, reported that he was performing the *putso* ceremony after over a year's lag.

CEREMONIES OF THE VILLAGE OR *BUSTI*

Annual Ceremony of the *busti*—Each *busti* in the revenue block is taken as a small, but complete, unit in religious matters and may have its own ceremonies. All *busties* celebrate their annual ceremony of Padim Rum. The festival takes place in the alter-room of any one house of the *busti* on a Monday, between the 1st and 15th day of the months of October-November. A spot is chosen in the alter-room, which is covered with banana leaves. This surface is then covered with flowers and wild birds; a fish, rice, and a bottle of *chi* is offered to the spirit. After this, all the *busti* members prostrate themselves before the chosen spot and a man officiating as the head recites the prayers on behalf of his *busti* members. He then turns to face the people and spits on them, thereby symbolically averting diseases and epidemics. This ceremony is followed by a feast.

Bhoom-kor—This is a Tibetan ceremony that has been adopted by the Lepchas. The Bhoom-kor ceremony is performed annually and is said to ward off sickness. *Boom* is the most sacred book of the Lepchas and most people want to own a copy, irrespective of whether they are literate or not. During the ritual, sacred books with a small image of Guru Rimpoche are carried around the *busti* in a colourful procession. The sacred books wrapped in yellow silk are carried by the women and the image by a Lama, with the entire *busti* partaking in the procession and ceremony. The pageant halts at certain houses where refreshments are served to the *busti* members.

FAMILY CEREMONIES

Sa-gi—Each family used to perform the ceremony for the spirit Padim Rum once every three years on the Friday of the month of October-November. This was a happy event and was celebrated from early in the morning till late at night with much revelry and feasting. Today, however, the Lepchas of Dzongu do not perform this ceremony and it only takes place in families that have a Mun or Bongthing as a member of their family. In such families, the ceremony is conducted annually and not once every three years.

CEREMONIES FOR THE PURIFICATION OF THE HOUSE

A ceremony is performed for Tsang-dong, the god of the house. The Mun decides and purifies the site of a house before its construction. The carpenter performs a ceremony, both before the construction begins and after the house has been built. The blood of a sacrificed bull or a goat is offered to the spirits, Dul and Cen, to ensure that there is no disturbance in the construction process. Lumps of meat and drops of *chi* are flung in different directions for the offering. Once the house is completed, the Mun purifies (*vyanhram*) the house with a ritual, after which the house can be occupied. A bull or goat, rice and *chi* are given to the Mun or Bongthing on the day of the rites.

The bull is sacrificed outside the house, after which the animal is taken in and its meat is prepared for the first meal to be consumed in the new house. The Mun then sweeps the floor with leaves and bits. Small pieces of wood are then cut from the doors, walls, windows, floors, etc. and thrown out, symbolising a ceremonial cleansing of the dwelling place. The carpenter performs a ceremony to his tutelary deity known as Mung Gum Rum or Mung Kung Rum.

Li Rum—The household also has its own deity called Li Rum who is believed to live in the house and shield the family members from harm. A ritual is conducted by the Mun or Bongthing in honour of this supernatural, which is said to protect the family members for a period of one year. A bull is sacrificed on the occasion and the meat is then fried and consumed.

Fung Mung—The Fung Mung is another spirit associated with the house and is believed to cause sudden and violent death by suicide or murder. A ritual is also performed to drive away this evil supernatural.

BIRTH CEREMONIES

The Lepchas believe that much before man came down to earth, God created poison and the elixir of life. He buried a devil and an angel and asked his disciple to pour the poison over the buried devil and the elixir over the angel. The disciple confused the two potions and poured poison on the buried angel and elixir on the devil's earth. 81-year-old Cheddamu Lepcha of Sankalang *busti* believes that since this incident, humans are born and they have to die repeatedly. The custom of burial is also believed to go back to this incident. She said, "Had the disciple not made the mistake, we humans would never have to undergo this arduous cycle of birth and death, and man would be eternal."

Bongthing Kenchyok Lepcha of Pentong *busti* says that he performs all the birth ceremonies in his *busti*. He described the details of the birth ceremony as such: The ceremony is performed on the third day after a child is born. The third day is considered significant in the Lepcha belief system, as they hold that it is only after the third day that a child can be considered fully alive and a part of humanity.[38]

On this subject Gorer says,

> For the first three days of life the baby is considered to be still in the womb... it is not even referred to as a human child; it is called a rat child...also, nobody except those who live in the house must enter the house or see the child.[39]

The ritual begins with the preparation of *lofit*, after which threads of five colours are tied around the new born's arm. A box open from the top is then taken and three stones are placed in the box to resemble the traditional stove of the Lepchas. After this, the Bongthing commences the ritual with the omnipresent *chi*[40] and rice and communicates with the spirit of the child. The spirit is told that it is blessed with human life and then the gods are invoked to guide the child's spirit in pursuit of its future soulmate. This is followed by a feast involving the family and the *busti* members.

DEATH CEREMONIES

The Mun worshipps the two super naturals, Mit Rum and De Rum, who are said to be ancestral gods who look after the dead Lepchas. Death is considered final among the Lepchas who perform certain rituals as a precautionary measure after one person in the community has been struck by death and the others are threatened. (Such beliefs and practices also exist in Lamaism. The ceremony Suneen is performed by Lamas to ward off evil in case of death and other misfortunes.) When a person dies, the funeral rites are performed along with the sacrifice of a pig or an ox. The sacrifice is said to be a present from the dead to his ancestors. The sacrificial animal is pierced through the length of its body with a sharp bamboo picket and the Mun recites prayers for three nights and days. The Lepchas believe that their spirits are taken to the local deities of the

Khangchendzonga through a bottomless passage. Each *putso* has a different passage and the Mun helps carry the soul through this route. The Mun worships the spirits considered to be ancestral gods who protect all dead Lepchas.

Burial Ritual—the Mun performs a ritual to carry the soul of the dead to *lep* or the place where the soul first resides. Cheddamu Lepcha revealed, "When I was young, Dzongu had many powerful Muns. Some Muns were so powerful that they could even transport the soul of bad men to heaven". She described the burial ritual as she remembered it[41]: "When a person dies, the Mun takes some *chi* and rice to the cremation area. *Chi* and rice is wrapped in a broad leaf called *kafer lop,*[42] along with the clothes of the dead person, a knife or *bum fork* (or a sword or *kum bun kup* in case of a king's death, and a wooden knitting needle or *tee lazyu lazum* in case of the death of a girl), a comb, a sickle and water is buried along with the dead body".

After the burial, the Mun starts to chant mantras. This is called *maree sung ko*. Then the Mun holds a live hen and a leaf called *pushyor lop,*[43] after which he releases the hen. A small wall of stones is then roughly constructed on the burial ground and two wooden ladders are placed on the wall. Two fire torches made of bamboo are also placed next to the wall in order to facilitate the soul to see in the dark.

The Mun then goes into a trance and invokes the dead spirit in his body. This phenomenon is called *munnyam kup* (or evil spirit child). During this period, the Mun's face turns a deep red, he/she breaks into cold sweat and his/her voice is believed to become coarse and rather inhuman. The dead spirit speaks via the Mun and demands for certain items like a chicken, rice, *chi,* etc. It is believed that if these demands are not fulfilled, then the dead spirit can harm the Mun and the family of the dead person. Great care is therefore taken to supply all that the dead spirit demands at this moment. The spirit also reveals details of how it was killed and who/what was responsible for its death. Cheddamu Lepcha said that this particular period of the burial ritual is so dangerous that at times, people have been known to die under the power of the moment. She also claimed that she had witnessed such deaths in her lifetime. The death ceremony lasts for about three to four hours and can take place at any time of the day.

It is of relevance to note that with the adoption of Lamaism, the Lepchas took to cremating their dead instead of burying them. As a result, these rituals too have been made redundant. Cheddamu Lepcha said that most people were buried till about 1960, after which the Lama practice of cremation became more and more popular. This practice was perhaps adopted because the Lamas claim that the soul of a buried person does not find peace and cannot be set free as it is eaten up by worms. She added that the death ceremony today, is performed by Lamas in Tibet and hence cannot be understood by anyone. She considered this a big disadvantage. She also reported that, "Today, the people call the Mun only in the beginning of the death rituals, to perform the *maree sung ko* after which the Lamas take over." The position of a Mun is no longer sacrosanct in a Lepcha death ceremony, as the pride of place has been conferred upon the Lamas. Ironically, the mandatory role of the Mun in the Lepcha death rites has today been relegated to a mere formality.

Cheddamu Lepcha also pointed out that the ceremony of *maree sung ko* was commonly performed not just by the Mun but also by the Bongthing as well. This seems to be a major shift from their ancient practices when the death rites were considered the exclusive domain of the Mun. "Today the Bongthing takes only about an hour to perform the death rites, while the Mun takes about two hours", reported Cheddamu Lepcha.

After the adoption of Lama death rites, the Lepchas have started the practice of observing Lama rituals on the 49th day after a person's death, and then after one year has lapsed. This is carried on annually for a minimum period of three years, though some families continue to hold an annual ceremony till nine years after the death of a kin. This, needless to add, is vastly dependent on the economic situation of the concerned family, as these rites are an expensive affair and include not only the payment of the Lamas, but a feast for all the members of the *busti* as well.

Adoption Ceremony-Adoption usually takes place when the child is between the age group of three to seven. A pig is slaughtered for the occasion and the mother of the child is gifted with the sacrifice and a new set of clothes.

AGRICULTURAL RITUALS

Agricultural practices are closely connected to the 'People of Mayel'. The Lepchas perform ceremonies twice every year in honour of this spirit. Legend has it that Mayel is an extremely fertile area that harbours all kinds of plants. The people of Mayel are said to be both spirits or *rum* and human. Lepchas traditionally perform agricultural ceremonies to Sa Kya Rum twice every year, at the time of sowing of dry rice and then after it is harvested. The time for the commencement of preparations for the rice fields is indicated by the call of certain species of migratory cuckoos, which are said to be sent by the Mayel beings. In this ceremony, the Rum Sa Kya is invoked for paddy; Sa Vi for millet; and Sha-rung for maize. Rice and millet are regarded as a family with the new seed of the millet being the daughter-in-law, the new seed of the rice the son-in-law and the grains are regarded as their children. Today, this ritual is not commonly practised.

One ritual associated with agricultural activity is performed in the summer, before the tilling of the fields to sow millets and maize begins. The ceremony takes place in the early morning in any place where the Mung is supposed to be. Any domestic animal can be used as a sacrifice for the ritual. The sacrificial animal is chosen by the Bongthing, who leads the entire *busti* to the spot where the sacrifice takes place. The animal is then killed by either slicing its throat or thrusting a sharp bamboo stick into its heart. A bowl of blood from the animal is then sprinkled by hand on the site of the Mung, after which the tilling of fields is started. This ceremony is repeated for all the crops in the fields that harbour a malignant spirit or *mung*. However, this ceremony too is not extremely common in Dzongu today.

This is not to say that people have disassociated themselves with their old practices completely. In fact, it would not be out of line to state that these rituals continue to be of some substance for the Lepchas of Dzongu even today. And, this can perhaps be best illustrated by the example of the cardamom goddess Elaiji Nyou. The need to propitiate the gods and spirits must have been such that a ritual concerned with the goddess of cardamom, known as Elaiji Nyou, was introduced after cardamom became an important crop in Dzongu. And, this ritual continues to be religiously performed every year by the Lepcha families in their individual fields. Muns and Bongthings also report that apart from rituals for illness, the propitiation of the cardamom goddess is among the most common ceremonies conducted in Dzongu today. Perhaps, this indicates the persistent superstitious nature of the Lepchas and the need to mollify whichever spirit is of special consequence to the coexisting Lepcha life. From Gorer's accounts, the cardamom fields had a structure called Mung-li or devil's house.

6

Behaviour and Morality

The upbringing of the Lepchas from their earliest childhood stresses social approval and disapproval as the chief motive for adopting or rejecting behaviour types. Lepchas are very unwilling to speculate on the motives of another's actions. Individualism is discouraged and a Lepcha grows up defining himself as a part of a whole rather than the whole himself.

Emotional outbursts are rare and they are seldom known to dramatise their emotions. They are famously lazy and completely prescribe to the oblivion of intoxicants like *chi* and alcohol. Jest forms an essential part of their daily lives and very early in life, a Rong learns that approval is sought not by self-assertion but by passivity. This is perhaps a key factor in the suppression of competition and aggression in the Lepcha psyche. According to Gorer, this might be a result of the treatment of young children among the Lepchas. Interestingly, he outlines two factors that might result in their lack of aggressive traits:

> From the point of view of physical wellbeing Lepcha babies appear to experience the minimum of frustration and therefore it would seem that in the first few months of life there are few experiences to evoke aggression. But parallel with this gratification of physiological appetites there is the considerable physical restrain which the babies endure through passing the majority of their waking hours firmly tied to the back of their guardian, and also the complete lack of encouragement which their elders give to their

> babies' earlier self-maximating activities and attempts to acquire body techniques and physical independence. Young babies get no social approval from their attempts to crawl and walk...[44]

Scholars account in glorifying terms of their qualities of mildness and truthfulness. Gorer singles out the characteristic of shyness and timidity among the Lepcha men and women, and holds these qualities, with the lack of competition and aggression, responsible for the lack of 'development' among the Lepchas.[45] There are frequent references of the Lepcha smug satisfaction with their life and pace and disgust at being ordered around, hurried or dominated. When confronted with these foreign emotions, a Lepcha will simply refuse to acknowledge them. They also seem to possess a keen sense of space and can interpret and respect the need for privacy and independence in others as long as a person carries out his social obligations. Especially interesting is the observation of scholars on the lack of extreme emotions among the Lepchas. Gorer writes,

> There is no absolute contrast between plenty and scarcity, between a feast and an ordinary meal; it is a question of quantity rather than quality. There is no seeking for ecstacy, for experiences contrasting sharply with the normal, no desire for sudden and dramatised pleasure or grief which will stand out sharply against the background of life.[46]

No distinct trait of hurry or greed is evident in work or pleasure among the Lepchas. The Lepchas are indeed blessed with the virtue of patience and during my time in Dzongu, if I ever exhibited signs of impatience and hurry, I was promptly enlightened with the adage "*hurry is worry*". Gorer observes,

> Except for shame, hunger and sexual desire the Lepchas traditionally do not equate physical sensations and emotional states... Speech has very great importance for the Lepchas... Besides being the greatest social diversion, speech is also the greatest social sanction. For through speech is produced the strongest unpleasant psychological sensation that the Lepchas recognise—shame; and shame is on occasion so unbearable that it leads to suicide... Considering the size of the community

> suicide is fairly frequent among the Lepchas... in every case the suicide has been immediately subsequent to a public reproof. It is extremely easy to shame a person... Verbal threats of suicide are occasionally made, but they are taken little notice of.

The reference to suicide prevails in Dzongu today; however, the threat is believed to be most commonly employed by young people when faced with opposition on the choice of a spouse.

On details to hygiene and the concept of physical beauty, Gorer writes,

> The disgust reactions of the Lepchas are generally low... The Lepchas consider, and correctly, that the Tibetans are far dirtier than they...women usually have a good wash at least once a month; grown men on the other hand wash exceedingly seldom... The chief attention that a full-grown Lepcha pays to his person is the care of his hair.... Other points which are considered desirable are a straight nose, a flat face, a fair rosy complexion, a round head and a straight body without prominent curves. Big eyes, small eyes, pop-eyes or folded eyelids are ugly; so are dimples, too big or too small a mouth, a protuberant bottom or big breasts. Particularly disliked is too big a head or a 'curved face', that is a face which in silhouette does not fall into one plane... Good quality and clean clothes and jewels add to the self-confidence of the wearer and to a certain extent enhance the wearer's beauty; but clothes and jewels could never be a substitute for beauty. Nobody would think of borrowing other people's clothes or jewels in order to appear finer and richer than they really are.

These observations still hold true. Ablutions remain painfully rare among many Lepchas, and the general level of hygiene, indeed leaves much to be desired. The medical staff in Dzongu and the local NGO, however, are working towards creating greater awareness in this field among the people. The idea of beauty is now increasingly shaped by a growing Western viewpoint and what they see on television.

Gorer observes,

> The Lepchas possess remarkably vivid and exact verbal and visual memories. They do not price intellectual quickness and it

> is, on the whole, not one of their characteristics. Numbers are practically meaningless to them and numerical concepts play a very small role...[47]

With increased literacy in the area, the latter observations are no longer precise today. (Indeed, it is difficult to say if such conclusions could be drawn at any time.) There is a growing emphasis among the Lepchas of Dzongu to educate their children and amass *intellectual quickness*. With enhanced financial powers accrued from cardamom plantation returns, a growing number of families are now also sending their children to study in better schools across Sikkim. This has been made possible partly by the migrant labour population. As of now, with the availability of additional help, the assistance of children is no longer deemed vital in the economic life of the Lepchas, and the children can be spared. Even so, a majority of the children in Dzongu study in the local schools, which have a high drop-out rate. The teachers here are of the opinion that often, illiterate parents cannot emphasise sufficiently on the importance of education and children are rarely pressed to study if they express aversion in going to school.

The Lepchas traditionally tend to minimise the most obvious contrasts like those between the rich and poor and even adult and 'little adults' or children and concentrate instead on the commonalities that bind them. Jealousy is, broadly speaking, not recognised and aspirations that may only be achieved at the expense of another are not given social sanction and a sense of morality and behaviour that enhances relative egalitarianism is appreciated. Nonetheless, a change may be discerned with the growing individualism, materialistic values and the increased monetisation of the Lepchas of Dzongu. A palpable shift towards amassing material wealth, and the ills that come with it, are observed. Today, a person who owns a concrete house and a jeep is considered wealthy and commands an enviable status among the Lepchas. The aspiration of acquiring a government job is also common among the Lepchas.

However, this is a common quest among not only the Lepchas but, unfortunately, for almost all Sikkimese people throughout the state. Government jobs are in great demand as they represent a lifetime of sloth, security and status.

Gorer describes the Lepchas as extremely unselfish and tolerant and ascribes the quality to their sense of contentment and indifference. He also talks of the Lepchas lacking any sense of inferiority in comparison with more favoured groups and individuals.[48] This observation is, however, refuted by the 'more favoured' groups or the Bhutias. The Bhutias of Sikkim in general and more specifically the members of the Tholung family (the official caretakers of the Tholung monastery and the only Bhutia family to have lived in Dzongu for generations) claim the Lepchas to be ungrateful and riddled with an inferiority complex and a sense of insecurity and jealousy. On the other hand, the Lepchas in the region profess a strong dislike for the autocratic regime of the Tholung family and blame them for amassing their land by foul means and extracting free labour from the Lepchas under impunity of the erstwhile Bhutia monarchy. The Tholung family, conversely, completely denies the above charges, although, when questioned on how they came to acquire the huge quantity of land they now own, they could come up with no substantial answers. It is perhaps of consequence to mention that I could describe my brush with the Tholung family as a telling one, for among the Lepchas I never experienced insolence. Their treatment of me could perhaps be described as mildly feudal. Appointments were often not met and no apologies offered for my loss of time and energy. I was made to stand and wait outside their home until the person I wished to meet surfaced and eventually invited me in. However, this opinion is only a collective one and many variances exist within the family that has perhaps been humbled by the ethos of democracy. One such member of the family is Karma Choppel, who is well appreciated by the Lepchas of Dzongu and is, in fact, a Panchayat member of the Lingzyah *busti*.

The Tholung family blames the Indian democracy for the growing 'communal' feeling among the Lepchas. This is of immense interest because this grudge with the Indian rule was observed not just in the Bhutias of the Tholung family but also among other Bhutias encountered in Mangan and Gangtok. The Nepalis and Lepchas, however, seem to be less inclined to blame the principles of democracy and, conversely, claim to have benefited under the Indian rule. However, they hold that even though democracy has made all the Sikkimese people equal, the Bhutias continue to be the elite in Sikkim because of their enhanced status under the monarchy. It was interesting to note that even the educated Lepchas working in government offices confessed feeling inferior to the Bhutias. "Bhutias belong to the ruling community. They used to dominate and boss over the Lepchas. The average Lepcha grows up with an inferiority complex from the Bhutias",[49] said Mr. N.T. Lepcha. On the other hand, the relationship of the Lepchas with the Nepali migratory labour population may be that of superiority as the Lepchas are the landowners and the Nepalis merely the labour class. Nevertheless, in my observation, it was seldom exploitative in nature. It might be worthwhile to mention here that I attended a harvest feast in a Lepcha family I lived with in Lingthem. After the harvest, the landlord, Tashi Lepcha and his wife invited all the labourers who worked with him on his fields for a meal. The food was prepared by Tashi and his wife and they personally served food and *chi* to all the labourers. I could discern no master-servant equation during the feast and, indeed, can only describe their relationship as an amiable and friendly one. Nevertheless, cases of disagreement in profit-sharing between the Lepchas and Nepalis have know to occur.

Some damaging shifts may certainly be recognised in the Lepcha psyche today but, even so, broadly, the Lepchas of Dzongu seem to have maintained their egalitarian ethos and it would not be out of line to add that their intrinsic principles of simplicity, equality, joy and hospitality have been largely retained. The Lepchas are indeed gracious hosts and they give freely not only their love, wisdom and time, but also their possessions.

STATUS OF WOMEN

The productive capability of Lepcha women is highly valued. The only male activity traditionally never performed by a woman is ploughing. Lepcha men, on the other hand, may, at times, carry out all the tasks assigned to women. In communal work parties, a woman's labour is interchangeable with that of a man and both the sexes are paid the same amount of remuneration. Even so, the social standing of a Lepcha woman is not comparable to that of a Lepcha man. The woman is observed to be subordinate to the man and most of the important familial, social, religious and communal decisions are put into the hands of the men of the society. The daughter cannot inherit any landed property from the father, although exceptions exist, her prominence in her original family is much diminished after she is married off. However, even though her contribution to the society may not be formally acknowledged and given its due, it may be said that the Lepcha woman leads a reasonably democratic existence and participates in the social, economic and decision-making processes of her immediate family and society.

In the religious domain, the sacrifice of animals by women is strictly prohibited. In fact, it is considered a sin to consume an animal killed by a woman. If, by mistake, a woman does kill an animal, she has to perform purification rites conducted by a Lama and make offerings to the Gompa. In the Mun religion, however, their existing belief holds that the female supernaturals are more powerful than their male counterparts. Today, however, these dynamics have been altered by the adoption of Lamaism. Some scholars also refer to the Mun religion's male-female hierarchy as an indication of the matriarchal beginnings of the Lepchas. Even today, the role of the male or female Mun is more superior to that of a male Bongthing, with the female Mun given the most prominent status of power.[50]

Observing the system of marriage among the Lepchas elucidates some interesting aspects of a woman's social standing. In the Lepcha theory, the wife is purchased by the husband's clan or *putso* and she continues to be the property of her husband's *putso* even after his death. This can be underlined by the fact that a widow can be remarried to another member of her husband's *putso* even without consulting her parents. Monogamy is the general practice among the Lepchas, but the levirate and sororate are also observed. Nevertheless, unlike Hindu marriages, the groom's family has to bear the greater financial burden of a marriage among the Lepchas and not the family of the bride.

It is held that there is no temperamental difference between men and women and similar standards of behaviour are expected from both the sexes. The standards of beauty too, traditionally, are identical among the Lepchas.[51] However, with the growing shift in the ideal of beauty to a more Western standpoint, the Rong girls today are subject to a completely new set of social pressures from the male members of their society in terms of appearance. Here, it must be mentioned that Rong men too face similar pressures from the women.

When a Lepcha child is due, the pre-natal precautions are observed by both the mother and father, but not in equal measure. Gorer writes,

> Both parents are equally capable of influencing the child within the womb, and in point of fact the greater number of the precautions to be observed are concerned with work which is liable to fall to a man rather than a woman.[52]

The status of both the husband and wife is believed to be enhanced by the birth of an offspring. Traditionally, an ox, pig or goat was sacrificed on the birth of a boy whereas no sacrifice took place on the birth of a girl child, instead, some meat was brought and served on the ceremony on the third day of birth. However, an ox could be sacrificed even on the occasion of the birth of a girl if the parents wanted the next child to be a boy.

A certain amount of emphasis is laid upon the 'correct' upbringing of a girl child and young girls are made to spend more time with their parents than boys. In the younger days, boys are allowed more liberty than girls are but the discrepancy is not oppressive. Gorer writes,

> A few of the girls—the tomboys—like to get away to play with the other children, but adults try to discourage this as a reputation for neglecting her work to go and play would tell against the girl's chances of marriage. The same holds good, but within somewhat wider limits, for boys.[53]

There is also a lack of overbearing possessiveness among the male members of a family with respect to the female members of a household. To quote Gorer,

> There is no overt jealousy on part of fathers or brothers towards the lovers of their sisters or daughters; and it is considered that men have no call to interfere in the sexual life of their female blood-relations unless an unmarried girl produces a bastard. Fathers will generally warn their daughters to be circumspect on this account when they think they have reached an age when this becomes possible; but it was agreed that unless a girl were pregnant a father would have no justification in being angry with her or the man if he discovered his daughter with a lover.

The casual attitude of the Lepchas towards sex, investigated in detail by Gorer, seems to stand altered today. It may be said that sex is no longer simply a casual pastime among the Lepchas. On the contrary, most Lepchas seemed to be rather conscious and inhibited while talking about sex. This shift in itself seems significant although liberal attitudes might prevail in the interior areas of Dzongu, but sex certainly does not seem to be taken as lightly, especially by the women. A girl in Lower Dzongu said that if her parents found out that she had sexual relations with a man, they would beat her up and then persuade the two to marry. The Lepchas might easily be described as more conservative today than they used to be in the 30s, as according to Gorer[54]; the influence of the mainstream Indian male chauvinism has undoubtedly left its mark on the unsuspecting Rong male population. Even so, it might be observed that the Lepcha women assert their independence within their domain and do not seem to take kindly to overbearing male dominance.

The age of marriage is observed to have gone up. The only doctor in Dzongu, Dr. Gyamtso Bhutia, claims that the incidence of teenage marriage is considerably lower. This is a major shift from Gorer's time in the reserve in the 30s, who recorded that in Lingthem, there were only four unmarried girls over the age of twelve.[55] Perhaps, this is an important reason behind the rise in love marriages in Dzongu as apposed to arranged marriages, as in the 30s the Rongs married very young. Gorer notes, "In by far the greater number of cases the two children to be betrothed do not know one another at all before betrothal."[56]

Marriage was observed to be a more disagreeable time for boys as compared with girls. Gorer writes,

> For boys betrothal is a much more actively disagreeable time than for girls. Between asek and the marriage feast the groom is in a more openly dependent and humiliating position than at any other period in his life. His parents-in-law have powers of compulsion and shame over him which his own parents do not possess; he has to visit his parents-in-law and help them with with their work whenever he is summoned ; incapacitating illness is the only acceptable is the only excuse for refusing a father-in-law's orders; neither personal nor family interests may stand in the way. When he is in his father-in-law's house the groom is under considerable restraint; he must be modest and circumspect in his language and behaviour and must be consistently respectful to his bride's parents and elder siblings. His wife's brothers have considerable license to tease him and to use obscene language to him; he must in no account retort in kind; if he were to do so he would be shamed... Even if he is on friendly terms with his bride his visits to her home are periods of

> constraint and humiliation; if, as so often happens, they disagree, these visits are likely to be the most positively unpleasant circumstances in his whole life. A groom can only leave his wife's family at the express permission of his father-in-law.

The practice of service to in-laws by the groom after *asek* has seen a marked decline. This system of marriage is rarely practised in Dzongu today and *asek* is followed shortly after *bree*. This shift is perhaps indicative of the growing empowerment of Lepcha men. Conversely, no apparent modification has been noted towards the empowerment of women in Dzongu apart from the general influence of education. Indeed, Rong women are now Panchayat members, school teachers and social activists in the Dzongu reserve, but, going by the descriptions of Lepcha women by Gorer, it might be concluded that while men seem to have certainly benefited in the past five decades, women have perhaps witnessed a slender loss of status. Gorer writes,

> Except that they may not kill animals nor perform lamaistic ceremonies nor own land women suffer under no disability because they are women.[57] One or two Lamas told me that men were essentially superior to women, but I never heard similar opinions from a layman. Various details suggest that there is a sentiment of sex-rivalry, but it only seems to be openly formulated through contact with Nepali or Tibetans. In specifically Lepcha contexts this rivalry is unformulated and unstressed.[58]

Gorer also describes the Lepcha women as more self-assured than her male counterpart,

> A women of twenty takes her full role in the group of adult women; a man of thirty is still somewhat bashful and is inclined to hide behind the knowledge and experience of his elders.[59]

Today, the traditional comparable status of Rong men and women has been replaced by a social order, where men are considerably superior to women with much greater social standing and power than is discernible from earlier accounts available on the Lepchas. This is perhaps a result of the external influences and a growing acceptance of mainstream Indian ideals among the Lepchas.

There is a passing mention of prostitutes by Gorer but the prostitutes mentioned by him are not Lepcha but Tibetan women, based in Mangan, who mainly catered to the transitory Tibetan muleteers. However, their services were availed by a couple of Lepcha men for the fee of one rupee.[60] It was observed that Rong women have not steered towards the age-old profession. This was confirmed by the above-mentioned Dr. Gyamtso Bhutia, who asserted that he was not aware of any prostitutes in the reserve. Nonetheless, passing references were made by some Lepchas on some prostitutes believed to be operating in the area around Dikchu and Lower Dzongu, owing to the beginnings of the controversial Tista Hydel Project in the area.[61]

Knowledge

LANGUAGE AND LITERARY TRADITION

"Apart from their mythology, legends and folk tales, no oral tradition of the Rong has come down to us. Their earliest written text, Tashay Namthar, is a product of the eighteenth century", notes Tapan Chattopadhyay.[62]

It is believed that before the coming of Lamaism, the Lepchas had a remarkable literary tradition of their own, but little of it seems to have survived the passage of time. Gorer writes

> The Lepcha alphabet was invented at the end of the seventeenth century or the beginning of the eighteenth century by King Cha-dor of Sikkim. According to Albert Grunwedel the Lepcha alphabet is derived from a form of the Tibetan U-med alphabet.[63] Some sort of literacy is absolutely essential for the practicing Lama, and until the Lepchas could be taught Tibetan it was necessary that translations of the scriptures should be available in their own tongue. All the existing Lepcha manuscripts of which I have heard are translations of the Tibetan Lamaist scriptures; it is said that some specifically Lepcha compilations of mythology and anecdote have been made and possibly some may have escaped the destructive zeal of fanciful Lamas.[64]

Scores of their myths, or *Lungten sung,*[65] have come down through oral tradition and constitute the rich and imaginative repository of Lepcha folklore. *The Gazetteer of Sikkim* mentions that it was the third Chogyal,

Chador Namgyal (1700–1716), who invented the Lepcha script. It is also presumed that this script was based on an earlier form but its origins remain obscure. The Lepchas have some possible explanations: they believe that their script existed even before the reign of Chador Namgyal. Some traditions mention the name of Thikung Men Salong as being the originator of Lepcha script. The Lepchas of Dzongu relate that in the 14th century AD, while hunting in the forest, Men Salong heard the voice of the hunting god Pong Rum. On hearing his thunderous voice, Men Salong was so inspired that he scratched what he had heard on the case of his sword. The Lepchas believe that perhaps this might be the earliest reference to their script.[66] But Men Salong is surrounded by considerable controversies, making him a contemporary of Chador Namgyal by some, a legendary scholar and an able minister of the much earlier Turve Punu by others. I was also told that it was perhaps a council of five wise men who invented the Lepcha script before 7th century AD, namely Targay Lepcha, Sayoung Lepcha, Gollay Lepcha, Duangrab Lepcha and Goring Lepcha.[67] They also related why it is commonly held that Chador Namgyal invented their script. During his rule, the kingdom came under a deadly attack at the hands of the Gurkhas. It was reported that such was the might of the invasion that Chador Namgyal feared for his life and is believed to have run away to Tibet. What followed was a bloody battle between the Gurkhas and the Lepchas, in which the Lepchas eventually succeeded in defeating the invaders. The Lepchas are then said to have gone to Tibet to fish for their king and reinstall him in his rightful position as king. Chador Namgyal is believed to have been so touched by the good-citizenship of the Lepchas that he pledged to revive their script and have the *Dharma* translated in the Lepcha as well.[68] Chattopadhyay observes that, "From all indications, this script was really the all-pervasive script of the Mawrongs from which the Limbu script developed in the seventh century."[69]

Some scholars believe Turve Pano was the Lepcha king before the coming of the Tibetans. But, irrespective of whether he was a king or just a tribesman, it is evident from the words of General Mainwaring that it was the Lepchas who controlled the area we call Sikkim today, before the Chogyal dynasty was established.

> The Lepcha language which had, hitherto, been the language of the whole country of Sikkim, which all Tibetans, Butias (sic), or others who entered the country acquired and spoke, in which under the rule of Colonel Lloyd, business was carried on, and justice in the English courts administered, in the character of which, decrees and documents were written and recorded (1876: xiii-iv).

That the General took to the Lepchas in a big way is indicative from the point that he married a Lepcha girl and went on to establish a Lepcha school in Darjeeling towards the end of the 19th century and also authored *The Power of Letters* and *The Lepcha Dictionary*. He was especially favourable to the Lepcha language and said,

> It is impossible that a people with a language so comprehensive; with manners, though primitive, so superior, as to entitle them to rank high among civilised nations, could be engendered amidst the wilds and fastnesses of the Himalayas. They retain, in so marked a degree, all the simple ways of the patriarchs of old, as to lead to the conclusion that they must have remained isolated ever since such customs were in vogue... The language is a monosyllabic one (though not altogether an isolated one, as it possesses in a degree—as all languages however primitive do—an agglutinative structure) and is unquestionably far anterior to the Hebrew or Sanskrit. It is pre-eminently an Ursprache, being probably, and I think, I may without fear of misrepresentations, state it to be, the oldest language extent. It is most comprehensive and a beautiful one; and regarded alone, as a prolific source of the derivations and etyma of words, it is invaluable to the philological world. It however recommends itself to us on higher grounds; it possesses and plainly evinces

> the principle and motive on which all language is constructed.[70] But like everything really good in this world it has been despised and rejected. To allow the Lepcha race, and the language itself to die out would indeed be most barbarous, and inexpressibly sad.

The Lepcha (language) has managed to fox many philologists as it does not relate in any perceptible manner to the languages prevalent in the region. Some scholars believe that the language belongs to the Tibeto-Burman family, while others have found its roots in the Austro-Asiatic family of languages. The basis for these conjectures and conclusions has been the similarities between the Lepcha and the languages spoken by the Khasis, Mizo and tribes of Arunanchal Pradesh. It has often been referred to as the 'mystery language' among scholars. General Mainwaring, who compiled a book on Rong grammar in 1876, called Lepcha as 'the most ancient language' and in its structure he discovered the system on which all languages were based (see above). It is now generally accepted that in the 18th century, the third Chogyal Chador Namgyal created, or revived, a script for the Lepchas based on the Tibetan alphabet.

The Lepchas speak the Rota, or Lepcha, dialect and refer to their language as 'Rong-aring' or 'Rongring', which reveals liberal monosyllabic character. The Lepcha language is indeed considered noteworthy for its interesting proverbs, similes, riddles and metaphors and the allusive characteristic of the idiom, so that the language appears to revolve around innuendo and a verbal statement is almost always a suggestion rather than an explicit observation. This has made the Lepcha tongue rich and poetic. Chattopadhyay notes a few sayings,

> For the oft-quoted saying that a drowning man clutches at straw, they have: 'The tiger bites one grain of paddy when it gets nothing'. Here is another: 'The toad sees everything as a leaf for shelter.' 'When there are fishes', they say, 'divert the stream, but when there is no fish, what can you divert?' 'When a big man abandons his principles, it is like the plucking out of the bird's

feathers and flinging them to the mountain winds'. 'Bad intentions and evil thinking of people in authority are like loose mountain boulders falling or ready to fall'. Their advice to the young folk is: 'Wear the silken dress of humility, never hand over your heart to a bad man, and find proper advice in the solid tree trunks of older men's thinking'.

Another outstanding quality of the Lepcha language is the wealth of vocabulary devoted to nature, making it possible to verbalise complex subtleties of the natural world. Perhaps the names for a variety of animate and inanimate objects were assigned collectively. The names of almost all the animals start with the letter 'Sa', names of various bamboos with the prefix 'Ta', and 'Pa' for different kinds of snakes. Hence *Surya, Suthong, su-chyak, suna, suko, sangi, sattim,* and *sahu* are the names of tiger, leopard, bear, dear, lion, porcupine and monkey, respectively. *Panu-bu, Pamol-bu, Palong-bu, Panul-bu* are names of snakes. And, *Tangjung, Ta-zyang, Tangar, Tafu, Talyung,* and *Takchim* are the names of different bamboo products. Such concurrence on objects of common use and importance seems an interesting characteristic of the Lepcha. Perhaps a fine example to elucidate the depth of environmental understanding of the Lepchas is the fact that Sir Joseph Hooker, the noted English botanist and superintendent of the celebrated Kew Gardens, conducted the first study of the flora and fauna of Sikkim, in 1848-49, with the assistance of the naturally trained botanists the Lepchas. They already had local names for perhaps nearly all the trees, flowers, grasses, ferns, beasts and birds, and what's more, they could even identify different genera of the flora and fauna of the region in an instant. Hooker's findings from his expeditions with the Lepchas were published as the *Himalayan Journals*, which maintains to rank among the most comprehensive and authoritative listings of the botanical treasures of the state till date. Another interesting fact can be observed on the subject from the 1931 census,

> The 25,750 registered Lepchas were almost evenly divided between the Native State of Sikkim and the Darjeeling district of

British India, 13,000 being in Sikkim and the rest in Darjeeling, with the exception of 66 who were employed, chiefly as gardeners, in Calcutta.[71]

Today, with lesser dependence on the forest and the vagaries of nature, the Lepchas of Dzongu seem to have considerably lost their grasp on this age-old reservoir of nature terms. Most Lepcha children in Dzongu today seem more familiar with terms like 'Coke' and 'Maggi' (popular commercial brands of food and drink).

As is peculiar with this family of speeches, vocabulary constraints have helped enhance musical elements in the Lepcha speech. Abuses are a part of everyday speech among the Lepchas, and harsh words and phrases that might perhaps never be uttered in most parts of the country, easily find regular use among these easygoing folks. Even so, the language cannot be termed as 'vile' as some old beliefs suggest. But undeniably, the Lepcha speech, besides being a soft tongue, is fairly euphonic as well.

The younger generation of Lepchas today seem to be more familiar with Nepali than Lepcha. But this is mainly true for the accessible parts of Dzongu allowing greater influence from the outside, in the more remote parts however, Lepcha is still spoken and understood as the first language. In *busties* like Pentong, it is indeed not unusual to chance upon a huddle of smiling young girls completely lost in the mellow harmony of age-old Lepcha songs. Then again, this is perhaps true only in the reserve of Dzongu.

Most of their ancient literary works, known as *Namthars*, are recorded in Tibetan script. The earliest written text, *Tashy Namthar*, also called *Tashy Sung*, is said to be a skillfully interpolated biography of Padmasambhava or Guru Rimpoche. Chattopadhyay reveals,

> What is interesting is that their pep books like Chyuten Munlom, Timit Kunden, Guru Chyo Ong and Kanthak Okday were written in such a manner, using Rong ethos, scenario and life-style, that it is very difficult to identify the foreigner's hand in them.[72]

The British abolished slavery and are believed to have added to the Lepcha sense of security and well-being. Gorer's accounts recount a Lama Jiroong[73] of Lingthem saying,

> Before the English came, he said, we Lepchas were harried by Tibetans and Nepal and could not settle anywhere for fear we should be sold as slaves; now we have our homes and can cultivate our crops.[74]

Gorer also mentions a Miss C. de Beauvoir Stocks, who made two tours to Sikkim in 1925 to collect folktales. From her studies and three days of fieldwork in Lingthem, she published *Folklore and Customs of the Lap-chas of Sikkim*.[75]

Meanwhile, the missionaries were not to be left behind. Before World War I, some books of Christian teachings were published by the missionaries and the catechism too was translated in the Lepcha script in 1903 followed by a book of hymns in 1911. Chattopadhyay writes,

> In time, Christian prayers in the Darjeeling hills started to be said and hymns sung in Rong so much so that the word 'Lepcha' almost became synonymous with the term 'Christian.[76]

But the zeal of the missionaries was soon diverted to the ever increasing influence of Nepali and the medium of spreading the word of Christ to the natives soon changed to Nepali.

The Lepcha-Bhutia alliance became prominent due to a common threat they perceived in the wake of the large-scale Nepalese immigration from the twentieth century onwards, writes Gowloog. Chattopadhyay adds,

> The Lepchas and Bhutias had already developed a degree of cultural homogeneity in terms of food habits, religion, and even dress to some extent. This emerged as a rallying point for these two communities but the loser in the tussle between the Lepcha-Bhutias on the one hand and the Nepalis on the other was obviously the Lepchas. The Lepcha land was not only alienated to the Nepalis but also to the Bhutias. And with the alienation of land the very foundation of the Lepcha culture and identity was shaken if not crumbled down altogether.[77]

Some noteworthy endeavours to revive the Lepcha letters continued and are worth of mention; Reverand Gyen Tshering Sitling (a Lepcha) founded the Lepcha Association in Darjeeling district in the 1920s. Sangkyol Tasso's efforts aided Imangsingh Chemjong to publish the Lepcha dictionary from Nepal in 1970. The 60s witnessed a Rong revival of considerable magnitude. A cultural centre was set up in Kalimpong by the Lepcha Association in 1967. This phase saw the revival of Lepcha songs and dances, and the documentation of Rong dramas and operas—based on their myths—that were staged with some success in towns and villages. Literary efforts in the language were also recorded.

The Mani Printing Press in Kalimpong also added a Lepcha section to their existing departments of Nepali, Bhutia, Tibetan and English. This is said to have helped with the publishing of the first bi-monthly newspaper *Mutanchi* that was also introduced later in Sikkim. The monarchy of Sikkim responded to the need of the hour and made Lepcha the medium of instruction at the primary school level; earlier, Rong was studied only as a mother tongue by the Lepcha children. Efforts were also made to publish books to a higher level of school education. Under the able guidance of Imansingh Chemjong, the Royal National Academy of Science and Literature in Nepal also published a Lepcha-Nepali-English dictionary in 1970.

The Lepchas of Dzongu persist in their need to carve a separate identity for themselves. This can be perceived by the simple example that the Lepcha men and women no longer keep Bhutia names for their children, but prefer to give them Lepcha names—originating from the treasure trove of their myths and legends. Here, it must be mentioned that the NGO in Dzongu led by Namgyal Lepcha has done some significant work in the field to endorse a greater sense of distinctiveness among these people. This involves measures taken to promote Lepcha culture: dance, drama, music and handicrafts, as well as awareness-building measures and activities that reinforce a sense of identity among the Lepchas.

FOLKLORE

Background

The folklore of the Lepchas unfolds a panoramic culture of a people with a fine appreciation of the good and the beautiful. The Lepcha god is Rum, who created everything out of earth and rock: the sun, moon, rivers, mountains, earth and everything that thrives on it. He adorned the empty sky with myriad stars and crowned the earth with the Himalayas. The awe-inspiring Kanchenjunga, too, was created by Rum. Thus, George Kotturan records,[78]

> They had a mythological concept of the world which excelled in ingenuity compared with those of any ancient people. The story of creation is artistically blended with the setting of their life in direct contact with the eternal snows. One could not help but admire the people who thought of such a wonderful beginning for life on earth... The Lepchas have shown a remarkable understanding of moral and ethical values which should be considered extraordinary for a small tribal people completely cut off in the lap of the Himalayas.

That storytelling was the favourite pastime of the Lepchas is evident by their unrelenting fertile imagination. Scholars relate how on cold winter days the Lepchas would sit around a crackling fire and narrate tales of their creation or simply laugh for hours together exchanging humorous stories while sipping bamboos of *chi*. Every village or *busti* has a number of legends based on its homesteads and nearabout places. Today, such idyllic sights are not tremendously common even within Dzongu. The biggest reason for this is perhaps the shift of interest to television and popular Nepali and Bollywood music. It appears that the young generation of Lepchas seems to have isolated themselves with the age-old tradition of storytelling altogether.

Then again, stories manifest themselves in more ways than one. During my time in Dzongu, one 'incident' was doing the rounds which spread like wildfire in the *busties*, and must be recounted here for its fanciful imagination. I was told that a child studying in Lingthem School was continuously visited by a she-devil who kept enticing him to follow her into the woods. She was fearful and tall and had large breasts that could be thrown back on either shoulder. The child is believed to have been so petrified on seeing her that he fell ill and had a fever for almost a week. During this period, he said that the she-devil appeared before him repeatedly. He claimed to see her everywhere (including his classroom) but no other witness could behold the she-devil. Even so, everyone seemed to believe the child's account. I was informed that such evil spirits live in the forest and are constantly in search of children who they entice and later kill and devour. The children in the entire neighborhood remained panicky for a number of days after this incident. This was especially true after dark when they ventured out only in sizeable groups and would be horror-stricken at the smallest trifle. What's more, this behaviour seemed totally reasonable to the older people.

But before we look at some of the ancient Lepcha folklore, it would be of consequence to note that there is an insufficiency of comparable data on the folklore traditions of the Lepchas of Dzongu and of those living outside of the reserve. This is perhaps because many scholars tend to treat their studies on the Lepchas as representative of all the tribals and not just those living in a specific area. Siiger, who conducted his studies on the Lepchas in the 60s says,

> As the similarities between the culture of Jongu Lepchas and that of the Kalimpong Lepchas are more conspicuous than the differences, I have not hesitated to treat them under the same heading.

Another impediment specific to folklore studies is that it belongs to oral tradition, which keeps it open to various interpretations and developments, and, unfortunately, these variations have not been recorded in any great detail by scholars. There is indeed a near absence of authoritative study material on the Lepcha lore. Its pursuit is, however, not the simplest, as explained by Tapan Chattopadhyay,

> Rongs are great story-tellers. The story of the birth of mankind alone takes seven days to tell and that also, during the loong ceremony preparatory to become a Mun. Only Muns should know the story in its entirety, others will have to be satisfied with the abridged version. 'Under this world is an ocean and under the ocean a twelve-storied earth, where live Itbomu, the Creative Mother, and her husband Debu. Their first born twins, Fau-dand-thing and Nar-jyon-nyu, are in secret love with each other. After them are born the spirits—Mlum Mukhyam, Sakyeun-faat-it, Saba-feat-Chamu, Suk-dum-ling-ming and Chi-lel, all of whom live today; Palyou (gladness) and Pakyam (joy); then Ta-lyang, Ta-kook and Ta-kook and Ta-kok—blue firmament; then Bru-nong and Jil-vong, Long-mu and Tso-kor, who are the forests in the sky where the stars reside; and afterwards, of course, the stars themselves—Tak-bru-num and Jit-it. The ocean between the two worlds is the home of Tal-i-nau and her husband San-go. Beneath the second earth are two big vessels beside Itbomu, full of water, under which is a big fire; this is why the earth becomes warm and wet.' ...

Chattopadhyay observes,

> One may be amused today to hear all this...(but) what hardly fails to impress is the beauty of the concept, where 'gladness' and 'joy' have found a place along with the stars, the forests and the blue firmament.[79]

Unfortunately, even the Muns of Dzongu today can barely recollect their lore in any detail. What's more, chances are, every time you hear a Lepcha lore you will be told a different version. Nonetheless, what seems evident is the fact that the Lepchas of Dzongu and those of Darjeeling and Kalimpong have some fundamental differences in their versions. And, while there seems to be, at least, a paltry amount of reference material available on the Darjeeling and Kalimpong versions, the lack of study representing the Dzongu account requires immediate attention by scholars working in the area.

George Kotturan's[80] study of folklore, unfortunately, finds little favour with the Lepchas of Dzongu. At times, the discrepancies are wide and need further exploration. By way of an example, let us look at the case of the mythical character Tamsang Thing, who in Kotturan's version is the hero of the Lepchas and their ultimate saviour. However, the Lepchas of Dzongu claim to not even have heard of Tamsang Thing. Namgyal Lepcha, of Passingdang *busti,* offers an explanation. He feels that Tamsang Thing was introduced in the lore by the people of the Tamsang clan of Darjeeling, who have written a number of books about the Lepchas in the past. "The Lepchas of Dzongu do not know of the existence of such a hero in their folklore but the Lepchas of Darjeeling and Kalimpong believe in Tamsang Thing completely", says Namgyal Lepcha. What indeed seemed peculiar to me was that the Lepchas of Dzongu not only deny the existence of their alleged mythical superman, but also of any other singular "hero" in their folklore. In retrospect, however, I found this aspect to be less peculiar than novel and a consequence of perhaps their classless egalitarian ethos and the supreme belief in the combined force of their people.

THE STORY OF CREATION

A version of the story of creation goes thus. Among the snow-covered mountains sat the God Rum and one day picked two balls of pure snow in his hands. From the ball in the right hand he created a man and called him Phadong Thing, which meant 'the most powerful'. And from the left hand he created a woman called Najyonguyu, which can be translated to 'ever fortunate'. The Lepchas believe that these were their first parents and all Lepchas are their descendants. But since they were both creations of Rum, their union was, unfortunately, incestuous. Therefore, their first seven children became demons. The parents had 20 more children after the seven devils. These children in time were married and multiplied in number and spread across the southern slopes of the holy Kanchenjunga. But the fiends grew in number as well, resulting in a clash between the Lepchas and the demons, led by the evil chief Lasso Moong Ponn. This led to a great conflict between the two parties and the devils employed a number of underhand ways to harass and defeat the Lepchas.

The demon chief transformed himself into a number of forms: tiger, rat, horse and eventually an eagle. But, the battle was finally won by the Lepchas under the able leadership of Tamsang Thing, the harbinger of good and the saviour of the Lepchas. Tamsang Thing finally annihilated the devil-chief, returned to heaven and the Lepchas rejoiced. The Lepcha New Year celebrates this victory, signifying the triumph of good over evil, in an annual festival marked by music and dance, a mock battle and the burning and throwing away of the devil's effigy amidst shouts of "get away, get away you devil". (For details see Festivals and Ceremonies).

The Lepchas of Dzongu narrate a different version. They claim that Lasso Moong Ponn changed 12 forms, namely rat, ox, tiger, eagle, dragon, snake, horse, sheep, monkey, hen, dog and finally a pig. They say that the pig was eventually annihilated under a tree called *Sanyol Chu*, or *Utis*—it later became a mountain and is visible from Lingthem. However, instead of Tamsang Thing, it appears that the fall of the evil Lasso Moong Ponn was realised with the help of worms called Pushikbuor Nyangbu that commonly feed on the *utis* tree. The worms are believed to have asked God (Rum Nam Dharnam) what they would get in return for their help.

God: "All the riches, gold and silver you want."

Worm: "What will we do with these riches? They are of no use to us."

God: "What do you want?"

Worms: We want the tree Sungru-Sunglok (*utis*) to live in."

God: "Ok, you shall have it."

Rum also created seven divine couples or the 'People of Mayel' who settled in Mayel—a (mythical) snowbound valley beyond the Kanchenjunga. These divine couples are said to be immortal who become children every morning, grow up during the day and become old towards the evening time. They are the gods of grain and the Lepchas pray to them for bountiful harvests and timely rain.

Legend has it that the people of Mayal would come down and interact with the Lepchas. But this practice was discontinued perhaps because the people are not as pious as they used to be in the ancient times. Instead, the people of Mayal send birds to the Lepchas every year to remind them when to sow the seeds and when to harvest.

THE GREAT FLOODS

Legend has it that the great floods came a long, long time ago. The waters in the rivers and streams began to rise dramatically, advancing rapidly towards the homes and villages of the Lepchas. The people ran out of their homes and sought refuge on two brother and sister mountaintops—Motnom and Tehdong. The two peaks rose higher and higher to escape the deluge. After some time, the sister Motnom felt that her brother had fallen into the waters and sunk. Anxious, she bent forward to take a closer look and, alas, was engulfed into the floods herself. The water rose high above her and she sank into the deluge, taking with her all the Lepchas who had sought her protection. The brother mountain, however, was safe and sound and kept his head high, while the people prayed for a miracle to save them. At last, the God heard the prayers of the people and sent a heavenly pigeon towards them. The Lepchas welcomed the bird and gave it offerings of *chi*. The pigeon drank the *chi* and subsequently started feeling thirsty. So the pigeon started to drink the floodwaters and steadily; the deluge receded and the flood was gone. It is perhaps because of this fascinating legend that the Lepchas still consider the pigeon holy and worship it with offerings every year.

THE LEPCHA TOWER

The story of the Lepcha Tower is another interesting one and is similar to the story of the Tower of the Babel. That some of the Rong myths are strikingly biblical (The Great Floods, The

Lepcha Tower, to name just two) in nature comes across. This could perhaps be a later influence of Christianity in the region. Gorer mentions the presence of about 1000 Christians in Dzongu. Frank Boa notes in his thesis that a gradual incorporation of ideas and tales takes place when the tradition lengthens and the cultural contact broadens.[81]

It is believed that once upon a time, the elders of a village met and decided to reach the sky via a tower made of clay pots. They started making this tower which soon rose to amazing heights, and two men started to climb up the tower in order to reach the sky. Soon, it became difficult for the village elders to spot the men. At dusk, the two men thought that they had succeeded in reaching the sky and sent down word asking for a hook to pull down the sky. The men below thought that they had reached the sky and wouldn't need the tower anymore. So, they simply removed the lowest pots. That, as they say, was the end of the tower and the men.

THE TALE OF TWO RIVERS

In the times gone by, two river-spirits—the God Rangit and Goddess Tista—lived peacefully in the lap of the Himalayas. One day, they playfully challenged each other to a race down to the plains to see who flowed faster. Tista took as her guide the snake king who moved straight as an arrow down to the plains. But Rangit chose to follow the bird king who meandered and stopped at every distraction and took his own sweet time to reach the plains. Finally, when Rangit reached a precipice, he saw his lovely Tista waiting patiently for him. Ashamed to have lost the race he threatened to overflow his banks and cause a deluge. But Tista implored to him and succeeded in calming Rangit, and the two lovers fell into each other's arms and flowed down the plains together, never to part again.

CALENDAR

The Lepchas have an indigenous calendar. They have adopted the 12-year Tibetan animal cycle and each person knows under which animal sign he was born. The Lepchas divide the year *Nam* into two seasons, summer and winter, or the rainy and dry season. The year has 12 months with 30 days in each month and a year as 360 days. There seems to be no apparent rule for adjusting the Lepcha year to the solar year. Some state that at times they insert a few extra days in the year, while others claim that they sometimes interpolate a whole intercalary month called *la-uo nylt* after every three years, in Hee-gyathang, one year is of 13 months. This *adik mass* (extra month) is called *Tafao Nyom.*

There seem to be different sets of names assigned for months by different *busties.* In Hee-gyathang, people start the enumeration of month-names from *Kur nyit,* coinciding with the celebration of the Tibetan New Year. Tapan Chattopadhyay describes the Lepcha time cycle as such:

> To the Rong a *saiak* or day has five parts, seven saiaks constitute a week, thirteen months or nyoms including the third-yearly tafa month between May and June make a year or nam, and twelve nams complete a cycle. The day starts with *la-krong* (morning) at five and ends with nightfall, *sonap,* at eight. It has the largest part of daytime, between two and six, stowed away as nam-mom (afternoon), during which every right-minded Rong will like to take a nap. The evening, *sola,* is usually devoted to chatting by the fireside, using *tangbor*[82] and drinking *chi.*[83]

The Lepcha Association in Gangtok publishes the Lepcha calendar annually and all important festivals and ceremonies of the Lepchas are said to be conducted according to the dates prescribed in it. The Lepcha calendar can be seen hanging prominently in government offices and even private Lepcha homes and shops. Even so, it should be mentioned that there is no Lepcha in Dzongu who has any knowledge of formulating the Lepcha calendar. Indeed, from my knowledge, there is no one even in Gangtok who can claim to have substantial expertise of the science. In my information, it is only Dorjee Wangdi Lepcha, a school teacher at the Tashi Namgyal Senior Secondary School at Gangtok, who has partial knowledge of the calendar. He confessed that it was actually his late elder brother Lha Tshering Lepcha, who was accurately familiar with the science and that he personally possessed only a sketchy knowledge of the same. The head of The Lepcha Association, Namgyal Lepcha, did not seem to be especially worried about the apparent loss of this cryptic science. In a matter of fact manner, he said,

> We have already thought about this. We made Dorjee Wangdi Lepcha's brother formulate the calendar calculations for the next fifty years. So the Lepcha calendar will be published without a problem for many decades to come.

Needless to add, there is an imminent need to record the science in its entirety (if such an exercise is still possible) or else, as they say, it might be too late.

MEDICINE

The Lepchas mainly employ two indigenous methods when inflicted with ill-health: They summon the medicine man who cures the ill by the use of herbs, or they seek help from the Lepcha priests[84] to perform curative techniques via exorcism and propitiation of spirits. The practice of exorcism as a cure is perhaps owing to the emotional support provided to the patient from the larger community—the sufferer is deemed so because of supernatural elements and is thus not held responsible for his unfavourable state. But, in my observation, there seems to exist a slight overlapping of the two traditions. It may be said that neither of the two practices can do without borrowing somewhat from the other. The medicine man may perform cures mainly with the use of herbs, but his treatment is coupled with the reading of mantras and invoking of the supernatural Tuksee Rum (the god of medicine men).[85] On the other hand, a variety of plants and animals form the essential accoutrements for the completion of all ceremonies performed by the Lepcha priest. A ceremony conducted by a Mun or Bongthing is unthinkable without these accessories. Furthermore, both the *Bon-ha*, or exorcist, and the medical practitioner are considered to be religious persons.

This section will mainly concentrate on the former technique of their medicinal practice, or the system of medicine based on the use of herbs and other natural substances, found aplenty in the surrounding wilderness of Dzongu. Curiously, there is almost no worthy reference material on the indigenous medicinal practice of the Lepchas of Dzongu. Even the otherwise meticulous and detailed study of Gorer, surprisingly, gives no reference to the medicinal practice based on the use of herbs. It is perhaps of some relevance to ask why? Were there no medicine men during Gorer's time in Dzongu? If they did exist, did they escape a mention perhaps because their practice was not prominent or noticeable? From the references to cases of illness in Gorer's research it could also be presumed, more profitably than perhaps the above speculations, that in the 30s,[86] it was the Lepcha priest who performed ceremonies to cure illnesses and not the medicine men. If this was the case, then it may be said that there might have been significant medicine men at some point in Dzongu but it is likely that they had lost their status in the society much before Gorer's arrival in Dzongu. In any case, during my time in Dzongu I found that the Lepchas indeed have a remarkable heritage in the use of medicinal plants and the practice continues, to a lesser extent, even today. It is also held that the practitioners of this school of medicine were highly respected members of the society; they would undergo a long and meticulous training period in the science and were addressed by different titles corresponding to their level of proficiency. But, not even the most renowned medicine man in Dzongu today seemed to recollect any of the formal terms by which they were earlier known.

The information that follows is mainly the result of an interview with the above-mentioned 71-year-old medicine man Tshering Badur Lepcha, of the remote Leek *busti*. Tshering proved to be a most difficult man to get hold of. Like other Lepchas he is a farmer, and not unlike some other Lepchas,

has two wives, who live with their children in two separate *busties*. He divides his time between his two families besides tending to his cardamom fields in Leek.

I learnt that Tshering was not a 'pure' Lepcha doctor as he had studied a part of his science from a Nepalese *vaidhnath*[87] in West Sikkim. A part of his knowledge was also acquired from observing traditional Lepcha practitioners like his grandfather's cousin, who was a Lepcha medicine man.

Tshering claims to cure ailments and diseases like fever, food poisoning, dislocation or breakage of bones, internal injuries, pneumonia, dog bite, snakebite, diarrhoea, dysentery, tonsillitis, cold, cough, body pains, and can conjure up a brew to extract still-born babies from the mother's womb. In addition, Tshering also functions as a vet and can cure animals of a number of ailments. Some commonly used plants in making herbal medicine are *kutki*, aconite, *jatamashi*, *chirata*, and *dhoop* (juniper and dwarf rhododendron). Some edible tubers, like the *kaching*, has medicinal use as well. Birds, horses, deer, musk deer, bear and wild boar are also hunted for the extraction of medicinal parts from their bodies.

To ensure that the secret of his healing potions do not die with him, Tshering has a handful of students that he trains informally from time to time.

> But I cannot divulge the cure of some of the ailments to even my most dedicated pupil; I fear that if I give out the secret of some cures the medicines will stop to have the desired effect. Nevertheless, my students will learn these cures gradually through signals,

says Tshering. When confronted with the prospect of the gradual dying away of such knowledge basis, he said,

> I know that this practice is dying out, but I will only impart this knowledge to someone who is really interested in it. The young generation is different from us. They are more attracted to the easy ways of the world outside.

Tshering also mentioned in passing that he was happy that one of his sons, Pemba Lepcha, showed a keen interest in his practice, and his two wives could also prescribe medicine for certain ailments.

Tshering Lepcha described the process of treatment as such:

> Besides applying medicines I also read mantras while curing a patient and invoke the medicine god Tuksee Rum. This ceremony is known as sur, and is marked by the burning of incense or dhoop, and placing a handful of rice in the palms of the hand while praying to the supernatural.

The most frequently performed cures by Tshering are snakebites, dog bites, bone repairs, joint pains, incidents of food poisoning and injuries. Tshering does not keep any ready medicines in his house and has to go in the forest to fetch the appropriate herbs as and when the need arises.

It is perhaps of consequence to note that the unavailability of ready medicines seems to be a major cause of the eroding of this tradition. His son and chief pupil, the 25-year-old Pemba Lepcha, agrees.

> Modern medicine is more convenient and easily accessible. I have been learning our indigenous system of medicine since the age of 13 and have assisted my father since then. I mainly practice medicine as an interest and work on it only part-time, otherwise we are farmers. Dzongu is so cut-off and we live in such close proximity to the forest. Things may happen when you are far away from any hospital or doctor. Our medicine from the woods works as a lifesaver in emergencies. I use both the hospital medicine as well as our local one depending on the situation.

Tshering elaborated on the salient features of the indigenous medicinal system saying,

> Herbal medicine is fresh and cures faster. It also has no side-effects on the body and in fact, makes the body stronger and builds the immune system. People who have tried both the systems of medicine say that our local medicine is better in the long run even though the immediate effect of western medicine may seem to be more fruitful. Bone fractures take a very long time to heal in the hospital whereas our local medicines can join fractured or broken bones, and the patient can go back to the fields.[88]

It was interesting to note that even Tshering Lepcha could not dismiss Western medicine completely. When asked whether he had ever consulted a modern doctor, he simply pointed to his missing ear and said,

> I was deep in the forest looking for medicines and felt a tap on back. I turned to face a bear that attacked me, tore off all the skin from my face and pulled out my ear. I stabbed him with my bum phok, or knife, till he let go of me and ran into the woods. I managed to walk back in that state and my family took me to the hospital. I stayed in the hospital for a month during which time the doctors recrafted my face from the skin of my thighs. After a month in the hospital, I decided to come back home and cure myself with my herbs. That was five years ago. After that experience, I have acknowledged the boon of surgery.

There is one Primary Health Centre (PHC) in Dzongu headed by Doctor Bhutia, the only doctor in Dzongu. And, although getting to the PHC isn't the simplest task,[89] the number of people prescribing to allopathic medicine is clearly on the rise. The reasons for the disappearance of the indigenous medicine and the increase in the use of Western medicine may partly be attributed to convenience as well as to certain indigenous reasons. There seems to be a discernible tendency to keep the local medicinal knowledge within the family lines. This could be a result of some superstition, a genuine lack of interested pupils or simply the need to guard the economic returns that such a practice could incur. Another reason, and perhaps a greater one, resulting in the decline of this medicinal system is the belief in the practitioners that if they pass on their healing remedies to someone, the curative power of these remedies would wane if not vanish altogether. This tendency was observed not only in Tshering Lepcha, but in the other healers of Dzongu as well. A man in Lingzya and another in Sungdong are known throughout Dzongu for their effective remedies for deep wounds and broken or fractured bones. It is also common knowledge that these individuals will not divulge the contents of their medication for fear of it losing its healing powers. Such beliefs further reiterate the aforementioned superstitious bent of mind of the Lepchas of Dzongu. True, this is changing but even a majority of the educated young Lepchas persist in showing considerable faith in such beliefs. Then again, it is equally true to say that this is changing gradually as well. Superstition could also perhaps explain the rationale behind the continued tradition of employing Lepcha priests to cure diseases. However, from my experience, it is very difficult to accurately state that the help of the Bongthing is employed more than that of the medicine man (though it appears to be so). What may be said by observation is that the Bongthing appears to occupy a more prominent place in the society as compared with the medicine man. It should perhaps also be mentioned that the legendary depth of environmental understanding and knowledge of the Lepchas, proven by the wealth of vocabulary devoted to nature in their language, is tapering dramatically. This could perhaps be another issue in the decline of use of the local herbal medicine.

From the prevailing trends, it would not be out of line to say that the days of the 'Lepcha doctor' are numbered—their shrinking patronage being one among other such indicators of the unfortunate fact. Imminent measures taken to facilitate easy access of medicinal herbs could possibly help in the preservation of the ancient science. A small nursery of medicinal plants has undeniably been set up in Passingdang[90] with the help of a local NGO, but, from my observation, the nursery leaves much to be desired. It contains only a small variety of plants and the available shrubbery is not kept in the best condition. It could perhaps be of relevance to upgrade this nursery to a truly functional one with a much larger number of plant species. The resultant convenience could perhaps encourage people to consult the herbal doctor. This may be presupposed, going by the general preference for natural cures with no side-effects as apposed to allopathic medicine.

COMMON CURES

Cough

Herb used–*Runkin*

Process–The leaf of the plant *runkin* is boiled and consumed a few times every day or may be stored in a dry bottle.

Cuts

Herb used–*Banmara*

Process–The leaf of *banmara* is squashed to produce juice which should be directly put on the wound. The juice of *banmara* is said to stop the bleeding immediately after use.

Diarrhoea

Herb used–*Tdungrhyeoul* (pronounced as tungshul)

Process–The fruit of the tree *tdungrhyeoul* is boiled to make a soup which when consumed, is said to cure diarrhoea.

Cold

Object used–*Aee-rungpuh*

Process–Consume a spoonful of this honey before sleeping for instant relief from cold.

The Lepchas install a piece of wood that resembles a tree trunk known as *aee-rungpuh* for the production of honey. A small plastic or wooden tube is inserted in the main body of the wood and left protruding a few inches on the outside, which forms the entry point of very small mountain bees. The honey produced by these bees is believed to cure man of 'all ailments'. I was also told that this honey is so precious that the market value of a small bottle of this honey is 'many thousand rupees'. What is clear is that the honey indeed has medicinal powers. I had a severe cold while I was in Dzongu and had a spoonful of the honey on the suggestion of my hostess. I must confess that I was cured by morning. Soup made from the locally grown fenugreek or *methi* leaves is also recommended for relief from colds. But, regrettably, I could not sample it.

WEATHER FORECASTING

Some old people in Dzongu can predict weather conditions by observing certain plants and animals. These techniques have evolved over the years, perhaps by studying the parallel patterns of different seasons with certain plants and animals. Weather conditions may be envisaged by scrutinising the state of a tree known as *sambrang kung*; its time of flowering also signifies certain weather patterns. The flowering of the plant *chyoungbur* indicates the beginning of the rainy season. Some old men are said to possess the knowledge to predict the timing and quantity of rain just by looking at the bud of this plant. Rain is also predicted by the appearance of certain lizards at the onset of summer. A ginger-like root called *munglee* or *munglam*, found in the forests of Dzongu, is used to predict the timing of summer. It is also said that in the month when maize starts to sprout and gets hair, there will be at least one heavy spell of rain. Predictably, caution from landslides is advised during this period as well. Some old men in Dzongu can also foretell the next day's weather by looking at the sky—density of clouds, intensity of sunshine or its absence, among other factors. The sound of thunder and its intensity is another tool employed in the prediction of weather by the people of Dzongu.

These methods are chiefly employed to predict the onset of different seasons, but are not deemed extremely accurate in foreseeing the time span and quality of seasons. What's more, with the growing estrangement from the natural world and increasing dependence on the world outside, the necessity for such information has declined as well. As a result, the weather prediction techniques of the people of Dzongu have fallen into disuse and only employed to serve as a pastime for those who still hold this knowledge.[91]

The people of Dzongu, however, employ the services of one Lama Apak Lepcha of Panang *busti* to postpone rains when such a need arises. The Lama lives in a quaint blue wooden house set a little away from the *busti*, trimmed with windows boasting intricate woodwork. He seemed to be highly respected by the Lepchas and I observed that people always went to meet him with small gifts. There was perhaps good reason to do so, for the 71-year-old Lama claims a success rate of 85% in stopping rains. The power of this technique is believed to be successful only in transferring rain and not in evoking it. Lama Apak said that he had learnt this Tibetan technique from an older Lama. I was informed that it was a 'Buddhist' practice and could only be acquired by Lamas and is said to have come down from a Lama who had learnt it in Tibet. Lama Apek acquired this power because he felt that the tradition should not die out; also, this would work to fill in for the persistent need to dispel rain in Dzongu. He said that he had taught the method of stopping rain to two other younger Lamas in Lingthem to ensure that the esoteric knowledge is carried on. However, he said the practice is considered an unhappy one and is, in fact, a *'paap'*, or an evil deed, because it involves interfering with the cycle of nature.

Gorer has mentioned a Lama Tafoor who possessed the same 'supernatural power' to stop rains and also refers to his uncle who can stop hailstorms. He describes the mystic exercise as such,

> The higher Lamas, the omzet and Dorje Lapoon, perform mystic exercises for the good of their soul and to acquire supernatural powers. These exercises consist firstly in acquiring the requisite instruction and then being immured in a specially prepared and completely dark room called tyang-gong for a certain period. While they are immured they naturally see no light at all; for periods upto a fortnight they fast completely; for longer periods food is handed through a series of doors so arranged that no light and no possible contact with the external world reaches the mystic. During the whole period the Lamas naturally cannot wash; a hole is especially prepared in the floor through which they can excrete... Tafoor is now the only Lama in the whole neighbourhood who practices the sending away of rain; his uncle naturally knows how, but nowadays he concentrates exclusively on stopping hail... Control of rain can be as localised

> as is wished; it can extend over a single field or the whole of Zongu, and can be held off as long as the officiant prays... The control of hail does not require the same precautions but necessitates the presence of some magical objects including a ram's horn.
>
> There is no question but that not only Tafoor but all the people of the neighbourhood believe completely in this power of stopping rain... Lingthem is very rainy and there were very few days in which no rain fell. In the last month of my stay there were six occasions when Tafoor announced beforehand that he was stopping rain and on those days no rain did in fact fall. The most extraordinary were the three days of the Boom koor ceremony whose date was fixed after some argument about a fortnight before it took place; when the date was finally decided upon Tafoor said immediately that no rain would fall during those three days, and in point of fact those were the only three days during my whole stay in Lingthem during which no rain fell.[92]

Gorer also mentions that this was the only instance of powers which the Lepchas deemed supernatural that was being used in day-to-day life.[93]

What is noteworthy is that much like the 1930s (the time of Gorer's research), the Lepchas of Dzongu today show the same intensity of belief in the powers of Lama Apak Lepcha and such practices. What's more, they can also cite numerous successful examples to validate their trust. From the above passages, it can perhaps be conjectured, yet again, that, like their ancestors, the Lepchas of Dzongu are not opposed to supernatural beliefs. Furthermore, it may be said that such powers in fact find prominence in their active imagination and they are not against prescribing to the successful supernatural forces around them. Another consequential observation is perhaps the near-absence of being self-conscious in their supernatural pursuits in spite of the obvious changes their society has undergone. The Lepchas of Dzongu seem to carry out such tasks with total belief and little consideration of what an outside observer might think.

8

Traditional Practices

Traditionally, when the Lepchas travelled to Tibet and Darjeeling in search of barter and trade, they also brought thread to spin and weave their own cloth. With the plantation of cardamom in Dzongu around the turn of the 20th century and the gradual shift to monetary economy, the Lepchas of Dzongu started buying cheap, readymade clothes from the handful of shops that came up in Mangan. Today, the Lepchas buy their necessary goods from the markets in the bordering towns of Mangan and Dikchu and some even go shopping to Gangtok. The emergence of markets provided easier access to goods and cheap substitutes began to replace a number of local Lepcha products. This in turn resulted in the withering of some of the indigenous crafts of the Lepchas. Some of their arts and crafts are nearly extinct due to changes in their lifestyle and decreasing dependence on nature, as well as alternate cheap substitutes available in the market. Nevertheless, some measures are being taken by the local NGO along with the government, for the revival of their ancient crafts.

The most recent such effort was made to promote the revival of the traditional Lepcha hat, woven from nettles of three to four varieties of bamboo and cane, by the Directorate of Handicrafts and Handloom based in the *busti* of Lingdong. The craft of the *sumuk thyaktak*, or Lepcha hat, had nearly vanished and was thus sanctioned a grant of Rs. 1.23 lakhs, by the Chief Secretary of Sikkim, S.W. Tenzing. One of the very few remaining experts in the art of hat-making, Tengay Lepcha of Lingdong, has been employed part-time as an instructor for a period of six months, to train a batch of students in the craft.

Other operations carried out by the Directorate of Handicrafts and Handloom are woodcarving, dyeing, carpet-weaving and weaving of Lepcha handloom. It is important to note that out of these crafts, only the handloom as well as the newly introduced hat-making are indigenous Lepcha crafts. The other crafts are mainly of Bhutia origin and the training in these is given to provide a means of livelihood to the people as well as to promote Sikkimese crafts. This is perhaps because the Lepchas did not have a very wide range of arts and crafts and, in fact, had no tradition of decorating their homes. Gorer writes,

> As a generalisation it may be said that the Lepchas possess neither arts not crafts, though they show considerable dexterity in adapting natural materials to domestic uses. Lepchas are capable of becoming very efficient craftsmen; the locally done carpentry work in the monastery is as good as could be desired, but such useless decoration is for them entirely pointless, an alien craft to be learned from aliens at the command and expense of the state. Datoop, a master carpenter, who had studied the craft for nine years and who had done the fine work in most of the monasteries of the neighbourhood, had not a single piece of carved wood in his house.[94]

A rationale behind the lack of objects of art and craft could also be the unavailability of a range of implements required for the purpose. Gorer notes,

> The knife is practically the Lepcha's only instrument. The knives are of iron with a wooden handle and a blade about eighteen inches long and three inches wide; the whole of one side is a cutting edge and the tip is square, not pointed. These knives are now brought from traders in Mangan and Gangtok; formerly they were got from Tibetans in exchange for produce... This knife is used for every conceivable purpose, from lopping trees on land about to be cultivated, to cutting up meat or wood for any domestic or agricultural task.[95]

The Lepchas of Dzongu still utilise the knife as their chief tool and Rongs can be commonly seen with the knife encased in a bamboo scabbard slung on one side.

The Lepcha sense of aesthetics however has undergone minor changes and in the present day, the more prosperous and inclined Lepchas enhance the look of their homes with posters, lace curtains, crotchet tablecloths and showpieces, and one can find posters of landscapes and film stars, torn out of magazines, even in some of the poorest Lepcha homes. The Directorate of Handicrafts and Handloom has also provided easy and subsidised availability of the Lepcha traditional dress for the Rongs, and most Lepchas own at least one set of their traditional dress that they wear on special occasions. The older generation of Rongs, especially in the remote areas of Dzongu, however, still wear traditional Lepcha clothes in their everyday life, though only a handful of people in Dzongu can still weave the fine Lepcha handloom.

BASKETRY

Bamboo is abundant in the region and is especially important as it has a variety of uses. It is the chief raw material for the local crafts. The Lepcha houses have a range of articles made of different types of bamboo and cane. Mats, baskets, hats, trays, mugs, straws, fishing poles, flutes and raincoats, among other objects, are crafted by the Lepchas for self-consumption. Traditionally, basketry is considered the task of men, although some women also weave bamboo and cane articles. And, as Gorer notes, "There is felt to be no disgrace in employing articles made by women."[96]

WEAVING

Traditionally, when the Lepchas travelled to Tibet and Darjeeling in search of barter and trade, they brought thread to spin and weave their own cloth. They also wove cloth from *sisnoo* fibre and nettle. Today, however, they wear readymade clothes available in the markets. The Lepcha handloom is finely woven in striped patterns over a plain or patterned background. The spindle is conventionally considered a woman's task and a small number of women in Dzongu can still weave their handloom. Gorer writes,

> Although weaving is now almost a lost art, the spindle is considered the typical feminine symbol, as the arrow is the masculine one; and in stories the heavy bar of the loom is the woman's chief weapon.[97]

It is noteworthy to observe that even at the time of Gorer's research, the weaving of cloth was deemed a 'lost art'. Nonetheless, it has survived total extinction till this day and now, with the establishment of the Directorate of Handicrafts and Handloom in Dzongu, the art is being revived to a certain degree and it's partial survival is under no immediate threat. The Lepcha handloom is being adopted to make objects of common use in the modern era, like bags and jackets, and a number of Rongs use these articles in their daily lives. Furthermore, the government network also ensures that these products are sold outside of Dzongu and weaving is made into a more economically profitable assignment.

CARPENTRY

Traditionally, carpentry was not treated as a specialised profession among the Lepchas, and thus did not develop into a full-time occupation. However, since long, the Lepchas have used carpentry skills, especially in house building, with the use of the knife, hand-axe and *ban* (a long sharp-bladed sword). Scholars mention the carpenters requisitioned to work in the palace during the Monarchy. Some Lepcha houses today boast finer details and require the use of more sophisticated implements than were traditionally available in Dzongu. Gorer mentions the superlative skills of the Lepchas in the locally done carpentry work in the monasteries. However, mere ornamentation without any usage was an alien practice for the Lepchas and seldom inspired them to beautify their own homes.[98] Today, however, the handicrafts centre in Lower Dzongu trains people in a range of crafts including woodcarving; and with the influence of Lamaism and other external forces, it may be said that the Lepcha aesthetics are gradually changing in favour of decoration and ornamentation. The beautifully carved façade of Lama Apak Lepcha's house, at Panang *busti*, is a case in point. He lives in a quaint blue wooden house set a little away from the *busti*, trimmed with windows boasting intricate woodwork fashioned after the detailed work seen in the monasteries. However, it should be mentioned that this was the only house in Dzongu with such elaborate decorations. It is also of relevance to mention that this is the house of a Lama and not of an average person, and thus perhaps more open to Bhutia influences as compared to the average Rong in Dzongu. Most Lepcha homes continue to be rather bare.

SMITHY

The Lepchas do not have a *kurwo* or artisan clan or *putso*. Nevertheless, one can find a mention of the Amzad *putso* that made agricultural implements in the ancient times. Today, however, it is the Kamis, of a Nepali caste, who create and sell tools in return for money to the Lepchas. It may be conjectured that the people belonging to the Amzad *putso* have ceased their traditional practice perhaps because they were considered to be on a somewhat lower social rung as compared with the rest of the Lepchas.[99]

CANE BRIDGE

The rugged terrain of Dzongu is marked by its precipitous mountainsides and copious waterbodies—rivers, streams, waterfalls and lakes. Since long, the Lepchas have lived here and employed their might and skills to survive in the relentless turf under the shadows of the Kangchendzonga. Their ingenuity and flair is perhaps most singularly manifested in the swinging cane bridges that dot the riverscape of Dzongu. The bridges across the tumultuous Teesta fringing Dzongu, and its tributaries of Tholung or Rongyoung that cut across the landmass of the reserve, are an ancient Lepcha art form with few equals. The task of bridge-making is jointly undertaken by all the male members of the *busti* and, if required, *lobus* or community work groups are invited from the surrounding hamlets for the ordeal. After the requisite Mun rituals, the task is supervised by an elderly and experienced Rong who accomplishes the most dangerous endevours himself and leads the team through the entire process—bringing down trees, installing supports, tying up the bamboo poles with cane fibre for the gangplank, among other functions. The women do not perform any role in the making of these bridges and only come in to supply the men with the much-needed food. The district government is gradually strengthening these bridges by supporting and running metal cables along their length; some of the bridges have also been converted into metal structures to enable vehicles to ply on them.[100]

A meeting of the elders and the young, during which various responsibilities are assigned to individuals, precedes the making of a cane bridge. All the important decisions are taken by the elders and the experienced. The cane collected for the bridge belongs to a sturdy variety that clings to tall trees in the forest and may measure up to about 100 feet in length. Extracting the cane is not an easy task, as the branches are thorny and the outer covering needs to be removed to facilitate the process. After the cane is gathered, the site for the bridge is chosen by the elders, depending upon the stability of the earth and its accessibility to the public and all the material required for the construction of the bridge is transported to the spot. A Bongthing conducts the prerequisite ceremony to ensure the task is accomplished without any mishap, and for the propitiation of the sprits of the forest.

The principle behind the cane bridge is similar to the modern day suspension bridges. The implements used by the Lepchas are mainly the *bamfork* or the knife. A tree is felled for the construction of pillars and supports and logs are transported to the two fringes of the riverbank, for the construction of the anchor houses. The anchor log is placed behind a sizeable boulder which acts as a natural check for the supporting pillars. Meanwhile, the elderly prepare cane ropes that are used to secure the bridge. After the anchor-lock has been installed into place, the pillars are erected on either side of the anchor-lock. The cane rope, acting as a suspension rope, is then shot across the river with the help of a blunt arrow, which is then hauled and secured on the pillars and the anchor lock. The other rope is secured on both the anchor houses as well, before work on the bridge ramp begins.

When the suspension ropes are ready, the construction of the ramp is led by the most experienced member of the work-team. He is suspended on a single short-length of bamboo from the main suspension rope with nothing in front to step on. This is perhaps the most risky task in the construction of the bridge as one slip could prove to be fatal. The individual has to slowly transfer his weight on the single cane rope tying cane ropes as he moves and hang on to the log while pressing the log forward. He is followed by a small team of young men who have to keep pace with the front man and make sure the bamboo planks they have placed are tied and secure. Each step requires a loop to be pulled from under the bamboo and knotted on the other side. After the most risky task is accomplished, the younger lot takes over from the elders and ensure that each and every section of the suspended bridge is firmly tied before it is finally allowed to be used by the *busti* dwellers.

HUNTING

In ancient times, hunting constituted a vital part of the gathering economy of the Lepchas. But the importance of hunting has diminished with the domestication of animals and restrictions imposed on hunting by the government. Though dwindling as a regular practice since long, hunting has been relegated as a mere pastime for the more adventurous and hardy in the present times. Traditionally, however, birds, horses, deer, musk deer, bear and wild boar were hunted for food, skin, fur and the extraction of medicinal parts from their bodies. The tools used for hunting were catapults and bows with poisonous arrows, while later, a small number of people also employed the use of guns. It is clear from Gorer's accounts that hunting was not a common activity even in the 30s. He writes,

> In the former times and still today in the less fertile regions, the Lepchas relied on hunting for a great deal of their food; but in Lingthem and most of the other villages of Zongu game is hunted less and less.[101]

The reasons stated for the above were the chiefly influence of Lamaism and settled cultivation along with domestication of animals proving the Lepchas with an assured source of food. Another reason was perhaps the esoteric rituals, sacrifices and abstinence that were a prerequisite for every hunter. Nevertheless, it must be mentioned that the Lepchas continue to be deeply nostalgic about their adventurous ancestors who braved the wild in search of food and a challenge; and even though such an act might seldom take place in Dzongu today, its romance stays alive in the heart of every Rong.

FISHING

Much like hunting, the practice of fishing too has faced a setback in the everyday culture of the Lepchas. Fish is used as an offering to gods and supernatural spirits. The Lepchas use nets, traps and fishing poles to catch fish. Bamboo traps are placed near green banks of waterbodies. The nets are made of cotton or *sisnoo* fibers. Lepchas also use the *hyren*, a line made by fixing a piece of wood at its end. The piece of wood swallowed by the fish sticks in its throat, thereby killing it. Fish is also caught by diverting water streams and clearing up the dried-up water channels. Fishing rod and line, *humsa sunli,* is also used.

GATHERING

Dzongu with its rich diversity and wealth of resources found in the forest sustained the Lepchas who lived more or less within the forest, and concentrated almost entirely on its resources. Today however, gathering is more an add-on to the main agricultural output. Yet, gathering still provides the Lepchas with ingredients of their daily diet as well as fuel and raw material for building and making objects of use. Gathering is generally carried out on a regular basis though, from June to August, when the food supply is limited, gathering takes place on a larger scale. En route to their fields, the Lepchas stop to inspect a variety of trees, shrubs and rotting logs to look for fruits, herbs, tubers and edible fungi. Gorer writes, "The Lepchas have considerable knowledge, for they know the edible ... properties of nearly every tree and plant."[102] Even today, the Lepchas get a variety of their most relished fruits and vegetables by gathering. While attending the inauguration of the Lepcha hat in Lingdong, it was interesting to note that from the available snacks on the table the Lepchas immediately polished off a big bowl of wild fruit popularly known as the Lepcha fruit, and not the branded biscuits from the market. Some of those present also put handfuls of these fruits in their bags to carry back home with them.

CLOTHING

The traditional dress of the Lepchas is woven in exquisite colour combinations. *Thokro-dum* is the dress worn by men while women wear the *dumdyam* or *dumvum*. The female attire is an ankle-length flowing dress whereas the *thokro-dum* is worn with an off-white pyjama or *tomoo* that reaches down to the calf. The male dress feels a little coarse, and is sturdy and durable befitting the rigors of life in the wild wide open. On the other hand, the graceful *dumvum* is made of a softer material and worn with a plain blouse on the inside known as *tugo-yang*. The women also wear a white jacket with a red border called *jermoo-tugo*. The Lepcha women have also adopted the Tibetan *baku* and can be commonly seen in the Bhutia dress. Today, some of the younger Lepcha women wear trousers and less frequently the *salwaar kameez* as well, while men commonly wear Western clothes.

JEWELLERY

The Lepcha women adorn themselves with a range of trinkets and jewellery. *Neckong* or silver hoops are for the ears; a variety of necklaces or *tho* with precious colourful stones and quartzes like cornelian and amber are also worn. Intricate charm-boxes of silver and gold, amulets on their neck and arms are traditionally worn by Lepcha women. *Leyap* or simple gold or silver necklaces are common among young women. The jewels of the older women-folk may also contain charms, inscriptions, hair of Lamas, bones, small idols, etc. Glass and metal bangles, an influence from the 'plains people', can also be seen clanging on the arms of young Lepcha women. But, it must be pointed out that unlike some other tribes, Lepcha women do not have any distinct native style of jewellery. Over the years, they have adopted as their own whatever gem or stone appealed to them. Men wear turquoise stones in a thread around their necks; turquoise earrings and rings are also worn by some of the older men in Dzongu.

9

Tradition and Modernity

MUSIC

The Lepchas are known for their legendary love of music. The soft and melodious music of the Rongs, perhaps more than any other singular emotion, reflects a contented and peaceful state of being. Lepcha songs are mainly dedicated to four emotions: love, comedy, tragedy and ceremony. Rongs also compose songs on the themes of marriage, agriculture, food, etc. The Rong musical tradition has nine ragas that are believed to have evolved and later classified from the cry of birds like the humming bird and hedge sparrows.[103] The musical legacy of the Rongs forms a big part of their socio-religious life and even the Muns and Bongthings, or their indigenous priests, render spiritual tunes as a part of their ceremonial practice. This legacy, however, totally failed to charm someone with Gorer's sensibility, who wrote, "To my Occidental ears all the music sounded like the cacophony of a zoo in a thunderstorm."[104] The legendary botanist Dr. Joseph Hooker, however, derived the quality of peace from the musical traditions of the Rongs, and believed that such music was a reflection of the unfretted minds and hearts of the Rongs.[105]

The Lepchas compose their songs in harmony with nature and growth of crops around them, and there is no fixed time for their rendering. Indeed, any occasion when a few Rongs get together for work or pleasure may be considered a fit occasion for their favourite pastime. The Rongs sing along while performing most activities like sowing, weeding, constructing houses or simply enjoying a peaceful moment sitting around the bonfire. However, songs are most frequently sung on occasions like marriages, birth and after the harvest, and never sung on the occasion of death out of fear of upsetting the soul of the departed. The musical traditions and interests of the Rongs have been somewhat influenced by the popular and well-marketed Nepali and Bollywood music. It is also perceived that the younger Lepchas, especially in the better-connected areas of Dzongu, are perhaps more familiar with Nepali pop music than with their own traditional songs. In an effort to promote their music and dance traditions, the local NGO, MLAS, organises troupes of students and performs Lepcha songs and dances at important events in Dzongu as well as those held in other parts of Sikkim.

A song about sowing goes thus:

> Cuckoo, cuckoo, 'tis proper time,
> The season has now come to us
> Time's for sowing, O cuckoo bird,
> Meet us halfway in the pass.[106]

Musical Instruments

Legend has it that one day their god of music Narok chanced upon a group of Rongs singing and playing musical instruments. So charmed was Narok by the complete abandon of the Rongs to their music that he and his troupe silently joined in with the merrymaking of the mortals. After the session was over, Narok revealed his identity and asked the Rongs to seek a wish. The satisfied Rongs perhaps needed little more than their bliss and took the opportunity to ask Narok and his companions for the feather crowns that adorned their heads. Taken aback, he gave the Rongs what they wished for, and along with the crowns, gave the Rongs eleven musical instruments to call their own. Before leaving for his abode, Narok turned and told the Rongs that whenever the godly demands would prove to be too much for his gentle soul, he would come and participate in the musical revelry of the Lepchas. It is said that since that day, the Rongs started wearing feathers in their hats called *yatpok,* which are especially worn while dancing; and they are believed to be so sacred that if a Rong drops his hat it is considered a source of great misfortune.

It is difficult to pinpoint the beginnings of this legend but it may be clearly said that there is only one musical instrument that is truly indigenous to the Lepchas of Dzongu—the bamboo flute. Traditionally, the flute was not played as an accompaniment with songs, but served more as a solitary diversion. In the past few decades, however, the Lepchas of Dzongu under the influence of the Lepchas from Kalimpong have added a string of other instruments to their singular repertoire. *Palit keng* is the flute, *nibrok palit* is a twin flute, a big pipe is *pantong palit,* while the famous *tangbok* resembles a four-stringed tambourine, *satsang* resembles the *sarangi,* the *tangdar* and *tangdarbong* are both small drums, *tangdyu* is a mouth organ, *nampathyut* is a small whistle-like instrument, *chakpanjar* is a version of a big trumpet, and *banga* is a round drum. Today, the Lepchas like to call all the above-mentioned instruments as their own. The tradition of playing musical instruments in Dzongu is not as common as that of singing. A number of musical instruments may be seen in some Lepcha homes, but it seems that these are used more for decoration than for their actual purpose. A number of Rongs in Dzongu, however, play their original instrument, the flute.

DANCE

The Lepcha dance or *alok* may be classified into six distinct categories. These are dances of nature, agriculture, war, mythology, mysticism and history. The difference between Lepcha dance tradition and that of other tribes is essentially that none of the above six categories of Lepcha dances may be considered singularly representative of their dance tradition as a whole, as say, the *chhau* is of the Santhals. The Lepchas usually dance in a group of girls or girls and boys together, and is categorised by gentle and simple hand movements and can perhaps be compared to the dancing traditions of some of the Naga tribes. However, the Lepcha dances performed today have adopted more elaborate hand movements but these cannot be representative of the traditional dances of the Lepchas. Some of the Rong dances dedicated to nature are believed to be an adaptation of the simple movements of certain animals and insects. Chattopadhyay notes,

> When an insect flies it is said to rub first its hind feet together once and then its front feet together once, after which it moves to the right, rubs its feet together, and then it moves to the left and rubs its feet together and so forth. Rongs dance in a similar way imitating the insects: their hands serve as the front feet of the insect and their legs as its hind feet. A continuous clapping, together with the sound of the musical instruments, accompanies the dance. Rongs have also dances in imitation of the movement of deer, tiger and other animals. Sometimes a dance is an imitation of insects, beasts and plants together. In such a dance men put on many-coloured, hand-woven clothes wrapped around their body, leaving the right shoulder bare. A sash is tied around the waist. The raiment looks like a pagi or the ordinary Lama dress, but with a lot more colour and brightness thrown into it... The most striking piece in the apparel is the feather crown.[107]

Agricultural dances or *zomal aok* are performed during the agricultural activities of ploughing, sowing, weeding, threshing and harvesting. The *zomal alok* is most commonly performed during the sowing of dry-rice or *zomal*. The dance movements and lyrics are reminiscent of a local myth. Legend has it that one day two brothers, both hunters, did not find any animal in the forest to hunt and returned home hungry and tired when they spotted a freshly dug grave. They unearthed the grave and found the body of an old woman whom they ate up to fill their belly. The two brothers decided to keep the act a secret and returned home. Suspecting something amiss, the wife of the elder brother said, "I smell some new flesh today, what is it?" The elder brother still had some flesh stuck in his nails and teeth, and gave it to the wife to taste, telling her it was human flesh. Consumed by the delicious flavour, the wife killed her husband and ate him up. The other brother found her surrounded in a pool of blood; he realised what had taken place and then decided that the only option left was to kill her. However, this was no easy task as she had turned into a witch. And typical of witches, she tied a broom to her behind and flew off into the night. The *busti* dwellers witnessed the flying witch and confronted the brother, who, shaken by the events of the night, confessed the truth to his fellow Rongs and seeked their forgiveness.

The witch is known as Lokkyo Mung (or an evil spirit with a cat-like body). Lokkyo Mung is also the name of an eagle-like bird in Rong mythology. A similar bird is called Konoongbong Foand, and the *zomal* dance is actually about this bird. The dance movements and the lyrics of the song describe the bird with a broom-like tail, fork-like claws, wings like bamboo mats and a neck resembling a flute. Her beak is like a snow picket and her eyes are like the *phengbu* or the necklace worn by men, while her head is like a two-sided small drum or a *gnarchung*. The dance does not narrate the tale of the two hunters but the Lepchas believe that perhaps the origin of the dance comes from the above-mentioned legend. The *zomal* dance is performed during the months of June and July.[108]

Jootyam Alok is the typical dance of paddy threshing and is performed by a group of boys. The dance has eight steps. The first step *kjyubu* is classified with simple leg movements and is performed with the boys standing in a circle. In the second step, or *karhyokbong jootyam,* the dancers stick out their legs at regular intervals. *Takchamchok jootyam* is the third step while *esyongalok jootyam, ungho alok jootyam, suhutungtam jootyam, popokoplyop jootyam* and *lamkor jootyam* are the remaining five steps and are performed by simple and elegant leg movements. This dance is performed after the harvest during the months of November and December.

Another popular traditional dance of the Lepchas of Dzongu is the *Laydong Num – Chyame Nyom* (name of a girl and boy). The dance is performed by a group of men and women and tells the story of origin of the Rongs.[109] During the dance, the girls hold a sickle in their hands while the boys have a bow and arrow and on their sides hangs the traditional Lepcha knife—the *bumfork*. It is an incredibly slow dance performed with boys and girls standing in different lines. The *Laydong Num* is performed during important Lepcha festivals and events, and is signified by simple hand movements.

ARCHITECTURE

The Lepchas are experts in building houses made of bamboo and wood. Being a high rainfall area, the material used for roofing is of primary importance. Traditionally, the Lepcha house roofs were thatched, but now the government is promoting the use of corrugated sheets to protect the homes from rain. Bamboo is widely used in construction and serves as timber for the Lepchas. It is used as rafters, roofing, scaffolding, matting, walling and flooring for constructing houses. Wood and thatch-roofed houses are gradually being replaced by *pucca* constructions and the locals have started experimenting with a range of materials for house-building like tin, metal, concrete and asbestos sheets and tiles. Traditionally, the Lepchas did not use nails in houses and secured all the woodwork with cane. Unfortunately, no such house remains in Dzongu today as the traditional practices of architecture have gradually given way to modern options. There is, however, a riverside 'model' Lepcha house constructed by the government, in Namprikdang, which serves as a popular picnic spot for the people.

The settlements in Dzongu are scattered on steep hill slopes, with houses often at considerable distances from each other, interspersed with expanses of farms. Only a few locations have a cluster of houses. The most peopled settlements in Dzongu, Lingthem and Hee-gyathang have the largest *gompas* or monasteries in the area and, more or less, act a focal point in the region. Smaller monasteries also exist in Samdong, Barfok, Pakyong, Leek and Sangtok. Small prayer wheels, or *maney*, can also be found in a number of *busties* of Dzongu.

Field Houses

The Lepchas construct field houses in their distant farmlands in order to successfully tend to agricultural work. They are similar to the regular Lepcha dwellings except that field houses only have one room instead of two, and are otherwise defined in terms of their location and proximity to the fields. The field houses close to dry fields are made up of bamboo matting while the ones close to cardamom plantations or paddy fields may be solid wooden structures. Some field houses can become permanent dwellings for nuclear families, in time, as and when the size of their original family increases. Another indication of the changes in material for construction is the use of plastic sheets. Large plastic sheets are placed over the bamboo matting field houses and secured to keep the rain away. The migratory Nepali population often uses these structures as their temporary homes during their time in Dzongu.

Details of Construction

The typical Lepcha house is rectangular in shape and raised about four feet from the ground on stone piles that go around three sides of the edifice and the east side is left open. The structure is made of wood, plaster, bamboo and thatch. All Lepcha buildings traditionally face north and the entrance is to the east.[110] The structure of a typical Lepcha house has at least two rooms moderate in size. One of the rooms is used as a multipurpose space and serves for a kitchen as well as a living room, while the other functions mainly as a ceremonial room. Some houses also contain an additional storeroom. The house is supported by five wooden pillar supports with a broad base—one in the centre and four on the sides. The access to the house is by a bamboo ladder and the space under the house serves as cattle shed. The houses have wide overhanging roofs that often jut out a few feet beyond the wall of the house. This is done to stop the rain from entering the house or dampening the walls. At one end, and often on two sides, there is a balcony made of bamboo poles tied together a few inches apart. The balcony is used as a space for sitting and also for preparing food, washing, dumping refuse and water, or even as a toilet for children and the ill, if necessary. The entire dump goes through the slats and is consumed by pigs and dogs.

The walls are made up of bamboo lath plastered with mud mixed with cow-dung. The roofs are usually thatched with straw, and pillars and floors are made from wide wooden logs. In a number of the newer houses with *pucca* wooden structures, the bamboo- and mud-plastered walls and floors have been constructed with the use of corrugated sheets.

Ventilation in the traditional houses is minimal, perhaps to retain warmth in the cold weather; as a result, the living room-cum-kitchen is often dark and warm. Gorer writes,

> On the east and west side under the roof-tree which is meant to provide ventilation and an escape from smoke; the device is not very successful and often of an evening I was half-blinded by smoke so that I could not see across a room and the tears streamed down my face. The Lepchas are completely inured to the atmosphere and could not understand why I coughed and choked.

In the Lepcha houses in Dzongu today, the living rooms have a window in addition to the the triangular opening near the ceiling which provides for, if not perfect, at least, better ventilation than is perceived from Gorer's account. The living rooms usually have one large window without shutters, to let in some light and air. However, windows are more prominent in the newer houses in Dzongu and some houses even have big windows draped with pretty net curtains.

The traditional Lepcha house does not have toilets or bathrooms, and the Lepchas use the forests and fields to relieve themselves. However, an increasing number of houses now have box-like toilets at some distance from their homes. Sanitation remains a problem among the Lepchas and although the concept of constructed toilets has started, the need to keep them clean and bacteria-free is rare. Bathrooms are constructed next to the toilets in a few Lepcha homes, though ablutions are rare and the need for bathrooms is yet not a necessity for many

Lepchas. Some houses also use nearby sources of natural water, such as waterfalls, springs and rivulets for ablutions.

Conventionally, new houses were always made in the autumn months and this practice is observed to a lesser extent even today as there is time to spare after the harvest and it is considered a 'good-time' for house building. Gorer writes,

> The intending builder gathers materials for some months beforehand. The site of a new house is decided by a number of metaphysical considerations. First of all there is a Lamaist book called Sachet Zai Putta which contains general rules of a very minute nature, indicating what sites are lucky, and what unlucky. This book is said to have been composed by four Gods who gathered together at Gyakar (perhaps Benares) to compile rules so that people should know which sites are good and which are bad, which fruitful and which barren, where children can be born, and where they cannot.[111]

Gorer has described in detail the myriad precautions and prerequisites that need to be observed before, during and after house-building, in the chapter 'The Homes of the Lepchas'.[112]

With the scarcity of land and changing attitudes, the intricate web of rituals and precautions described by Gorer seem to be given somewhat less emphasis by the Lepchas of today. However, the people remain highly superstitious and continue to consult Lamas in the process of house building; and some symbolic Lamaist good luck symbols and motifs that ward off evil can be seen outside every Lepcha house.

Lepchas are traditionally expert builders and there was no specialisation in construction works, as all Lepchas could build their own homes with the help of friends and neighbours who would readily come to help. On the unspecialised and community nature of the job, Gorer notes,

> Men, women and children all work together, and the task proceeds in a rather haphazard fashion, to the accompaniment of a constant fore of jokes most of them obscene. When the work is finished all those who have helped are given a feast.[113]

Today, however, labour is commonly employed for the construction of homes though in the remote parts of Dzongu, or among the poor, families also construct their own dwellings. However, the average Lepcha house today has more rooms, though they are smaller in size and the kitchen is constructed as an outhouse and is no longer the multi-purpose room it traditionally was. The kitchen, however, is among the biggest rooms and is lined with benches or raised sitting areas, and serves as the dining room and partially as a living room. It is interesting to note that even in modern houses in the reserve today, the kitchen is always a smoky wooden structure and retains the essence of traditional Lepcha homes; it is easily the most atmospheric room in the existing Lepcha houses. Bedrooms are constructed separately, with the main building of the house.

Some houses in Dzongu are also embellished with intricate woodwork. However, this is mainly a Bhutia influence as the carving on houses seems to be inspired by the woodwork seen in the monasteries in Dzongu and thus is not an indigenous practice. It might be interesting to note that the house I saw with the most decorated façade and windows was that of a Lama and not of an ordinary person. Gorer writes,

> With the exception of the altar and of a couple of the biggest houses which have rough coloured frescos on the external plaster and slightly carved doorways and windows, Lepcha houses are entirely unornamented within and without.

This observation still holds true to an extent; however, one can see some posters and pictures of Bollywood stars even in poor Lepcha homes today.

The traditional Lepcha houses do not have nails and sections are secured with cane. However, typical traditional Lepcha houses are no longer constructed in Dzongu although many houses with a fusion of their traditional architectural practices and modern influences can be commonly seen in the reserve.

Material

The wood used for construction of houses is of the locally available *katus* and *utis* varieties. The traditional Lepcha house is mainly constructed from bamboo and wood. Earlier on, there were only thatch-roofed houses in Dzongu, but the locals have started using a range of materials for house-building available in exchange of money from the Mangan market like tin, concrete, metal and asbestos sheets and tiles.

A traditional Lepchas house does not have any furniture. The kitchen stove is a platform of earth on which some large stones are placed as support for the cooking pot made of copper or brass. Earthenware utensils are not made locally and are, therefore, not used by the Lepchas. Other home furnishings are also limited. The Lepchas squat on the dung floors, but also use wooden slabs, leather pieces and animal pelts for sitting. Circular grindstones or mortar and pestle are kept adjacent to homes for husking and grinding of grains. Some furniture can now be commonly found in a number of Lepcha dwellings. The Lepchas make beautiful cane and bamboo stools topped with leather and fur, and basic wooden chairs and tables can also be found in an increasing number of homes. Plastic chairs brought from the Mangan market can also be seen in some Lepcha homes.

Looking at the changes in the local architecture of the Lepchas of Dzongu and the growing dependence on materials and labour from outside might perhaps come to mean that basic needs can no longer be met locally. It also perhaps follows that the legacy of the self-sufficient Lepcha *busties* is nearing a closure. The traditional architecture with the use of local materials is being replaced with foreign materials and thus money and markets for the fulfilment of needs. Gradually, the people are getting detached from their natural environment; and the land which gave them homes and food for free, now seems further removed.

ECONOMY

Mangan, the district headquarters of the North District of Sikkim, calls itself the '*Large Cardamom Capital of the World*'. A painted billboard with the catchphrase confronts every visitor on his way to the district capital. Opposite the town lies the Lepcha reserve of Dzongu. About a century ago, however, there was no cardamom grown in the area. The Lepchas of Dzongu mainly subsisted on primitive slash and burn farming techniques, enhanced with hunting, fishing and gathering. A more settled form of agriculture gradually replaced this order till wet-rice farming and cardamom was introduced in the area by the Nepali immigrant labourers.[114] The Lepchas adopted this lucrative cash crop which gradually enhanced and transformed their economic lives and resulted in the emergence of a market in Mangan with a handful of shops run by Marwari traders, who came to control the cardamom trade in the region. As Mangan is presently recovering from the recent elaborate celebrations held to mark the town's centenary (November 2003), it is perhaps of timely consequence to state that Mangan would not have come into existence without the presence of its rural, picturesque neighbour—the Lepcha reserve of Dzongu. Today, the reserve is Sikkim's largest cardamom-producing region.

The Lepchas are mainly agriculturalists and more than 90% of the Lepcha households are engaged in cultivation. Another 4 to 5 percent are in government service, working as school teachers and forest guards. Some households partially depend on activities such as construction contracts, running daily jeep services in and out of Dzongu and rendering religious services. There is no industry in Dzongu and neither any industrial training for the people, with the exception of a government-run handicrafts centre. Rongs are now a part of the monetary economy and they sell their produce of cardamom, rice and other vegetables and crops in the Mangan market in exchange of money. The Lepchas are known to have suffered large-scale exploitation at the hands of the Marwari traders and moneylenders of Mangan. The traders are believed to have been given the monopoly over this trade by the then ruling monarchy.[115] Today, however, the government organises fair-price auctions in the district headquarters during the harvest season to facilitate the Lepcha farmers. The presence of money today forms the fundamental economic basis in the lives of the Rongs. Small-scale trading is a vital source of supplementary income as well. Minor trading like selling eggs, *chi*, meat, vegetables and honey are important trading and exchange resources employed by the Lepchas. Economic returns from animal husbandry are high, however wealth is no longer measured by the number of oxen in a family but by the possession of material goods—a car, jeep, a concrete house or 'building', and most decidedly a government job with its assurance of a lifetime of security and sloth.

The Lepchas are increasingly earning their living through non-traditional methods like teaching, running shops and working in organisations and offices in Mangan, and to a lesser extent in Gangtok. However, cardamom plantation predominates as the chief source of income for the Rongs of Dzongu and in spite of being known as 'poor agriculturists', the attachment to their land forms the basis of their security and well-being. Their skills, resource and specialist production revolve around agriculture, though their workload has largely been taken over by the immigrant Nepali labourers. This has also enabled the Lepchas to spare their children from agricultural activities and pursue education. Conversely, they are losing their expertise in the field and are becoming increasingly dependent of the immigrant labourers. Gowloog notes,

> Today, more than 60 per cent of the irrigated land (in Lingthem) is cultivated by the share-croppers from Nepal on adhia basis in which the produce is divided into equal halves between the landlord and the tenant though the former contributes nothing but half of the seeds required for the next season. Even the cardamom fields are mostly leased out on adhia system to the same stock of seasonal labourers from Nepal.[116]

Another significant fallout of this dependence is the resultant sloth among the Lepchas as returns are ensured without even lifting a finger on the basis of the prevalent *adhia* system (equal division of produce) in Dzongu. Gowloog points out that the Lepchas have "almost completely abandoned the work in the fields to the care of the Nepali workers". Exceptions to this rule are to be found only in the Noom and Panung hamlets, where most of the households are still self-reliant in these matters.[117] The above observation in my knowledge is not completely true as I witnessed several families even in Lingthem, which was Gowloog area of study, to be immersed in agricultural activities. The case of Pentong should also be mentioned as most of the households in the *busti* are mainly reliant on their families and the help of labourers is sought only on rare occasions, and mainly during the harvesting of cardamom. The members of such households work hard and long everyday and only get to rest late in the evening when the numerous household and agricultural chores have been accomplished.

Slash and burn cultivation is no longer practised, as clearing of forests has been barred by the forest authorities. The land in Dzongu is precipitous and rocky and the initial clearing of the forestland is described to be an arduous task. The clearing was done by both men and women. The small saplings were cleared with *bahur* or a sickle, and rocks dug out and the ground levelled. *Lobus,* or community labour groups, were traditionally organised for additional labour, but now labourers can easily be hired in exchange of money or a percentage of the produce. Even so, *lobos* continue to be organised for crops other than cardamom, and some significant economic exchanges between friends and family take place in a ceremonial context in the form of gifts. Relatives asked to help in communal work are paid in food and later their labour is reciprocated.

Cardamom rhizomes are planted every five to ten years, and require little labour except weeding and harvesting. The harvesting of cardamom, however, is a difficult task as the cardamom fields are infested with leeches, snakes and an insect locally known as *bhusna,* which delivers a vicious bite. Snakebites are rare, but when such an incident does take place, the consequence is often the death of the person. *Bhusna* is also known to be the cause of some painful skin problems, while cardamom emulsions is said to be a certain cause of asthma.

Dry cultivation is extremely rare today and only found in the remote sections of the reserve. Animals or large implements are not used in dry cultivation. The tools used are the chopping knife, sickle, dibbling stick, small hoe for weeding and a special sickle for harvesting. The only inputs are seeds and human labour. Ploughing is done only on large terraces with a pair of bullocks pulling a wooden wedge shaped plough in front of which a pointed metal ploughshare is fixed.

In the recent years, the production of cardamom has been adversely affected by a disease that spelt large-scale devastation for some farmers this year (2003). Some families claim that they have lost over 95% of their produce to the disease and have no other means with which to support themselves. The Sikkim government officials claim that they are aware of the recent plight of the farmers and plan to aid them by organising to plant new cardamom saplings across the north district. The government also has long-term plans of converting the entire north district into an organic region. The district authorities say that this does not mean that the farmers will suffer a loss of yield, as their intention is to conduct the switch in a highly specialised manner and use top of the shelf techniques and expertise that would ensure that the yield does not suffer. However, the successful implementation of these plans remains to be seen.

Novel non-traditional means of income might yet enter the economy of Dzongu. The reserve might shortly be opened to tourism! The local NGO, MLTS, has done some preliminary research and discussions on launching 'eco-tourism' in the reserve. The endeavour is to make this introduction in a manner that does not disturb the socio-cultural dynamics of the Lepchas. They plan to initiate tourists in Dzongu as houseguests, thereby restricting their number and movement within the reserve. However, little substantial research seems to have gone into the matter and the people seem unacquainted with the spiralling impact of introducing isolated areas and people to tourist hordes.

TRADE AND BARTER

Until some years ago, cardamom was taken to Mangan and sold, and other household items brought from the Marwari shops at Mangan. Before the planting of cardamom, there were no shops in Mangan and the Lepchas had to travel long distances in search of salt and other necessary goods. They used to barter minor forest produce and surplus crop, if any, at the Tibetan border. In exchange, the Tibetans brought dyes extracted from some roots found in the forest for dyeing carpets. The Lepchas exchanged salt for cloth and thread at Darjeeling. To convenience trading on these hazardous journeys and receive food and shelter on their odyssey, the Lepchas had established institutional friendship, or *ingzong*, on a group basis, with the Tibetans and Nepalese. This bond was established with the exchange of intestines of pigs killed and sacrificed in honour of the gods for the occasion. Feasting and exchange of swearing on eternal friendship followed the sacrifice.

Obligatory gift and labour transactions among friends and families are important in the lives of the inter-dependant Lepchas even today. Small-scale trading is a vital source of supplementary income. Animal husbandry and minor trading like the selling of eggs, *chi*, meat, vegetables, honey are other important trading and exchange resources employed by the Lepchas.

Chukmoo Lepcha, better known as *azi* or mother, of the Passingdang *busti*, is known in the surrounding hamlets for her excellent preparation of the intoxicants *chi* and *roxy*. Although she was busy preparing large quantities of *chi* for the impending marriage of one of her sons, there was always enough *chi* in her house to serve guests or sell to the *busti* folk. I frequently witnessed other small-scale transactions between men and women mainly buying or selling vegetables and tomatoes from their neighbours and *bust* folk. The most lucrative transactions of this nature were perhaps the buying and selling of roosters and other meat products. The Lepchas of Dzongu seem to prefer locally bred products than their counterparts in the market, claiming the *busti* products to be superior to anything available in the market—be it tomatoes, fish, chicken or *chi*. This claim in my experience was not a far-fetched one, as the *busti* commodities were indeed richer in flavour. These small-scale transactions tend to be of an informal nature and often the amount of monetary return is left to the discretion of the buyer; and the sum is generally accepted gracefully without any fuss. Conversely, it was observed that the payee seems to be aware of his advantage and, therefore, extremely cautious of offering a fair sum. It was of interest to observe that the intent of exploitation or cheating was not observed in any transaction and perhaps is a reflection of the Lepcha ethos of exchange and fair play.

Money-oriented system

Traditionally, there was no money in the Lepcha society and there is no word for money in their language. Wealth was measured by the availability of labour fource in their immediate family. In the absence of specialisation of labour and a constant need for additional hands, such mutual exchanges become fundamental not only to unite the community, but also to accomplish tasks which would otherwise be outside the realm of a household. Cash entered the Dzongu economy with the introduction of cardamom and today the presence of money forms an important economic basis in the lives of the Lepchas. Today, the need for additional labour can easily be fulfilled by hiring labour. Their traditional practices, however, stand somewhat altered with the introduction of money.

DIET

The traditional staple food of the Lepchas is dry rice or *zomal*, *mongku* or buckwheat *roti* or bread, millet or *korhuku* and wheat *roti* or *kokyoku*. Maize is locally cultivated but considered the poor man's diet and is not really savored by the Lepchas; but it forms a part of their diet, and a snack of beaten maize is consumed by the Lepchas as well. Nowadays, the Lepchas also commonly eat wet rice, but people living in the remote reaches of Dzongu still subsist on the locally grown dry rice and buckwheat bread. Wet rice is more commonly eaten in *busties* like Lingthem and Heegyathang where it is locally cultivated, or in households that have paddy fields.

Like most tribal communities, food plays an extremely important role in the physical and emotional well-being of the Rongs, and much of their social and cultural life is centred around the consumption of large quantities of food and *chi*. Gorer writes,

> Love, whether between spouses, friends, or parents and children, is considered to be the result of mutual benefits, and foremost among these mutual benefits is the gathering and preparation of food. For Lepchas, love is never automatic; if they say they love a person they will always explain why they do so. Even with young children this attitude is firmly implanted; if you ask one if he loves his parents he will almost certainly reply 'I love my mother and father because they give me food.'... Rigya, a young man, ... has been fairly recently married and at first he and his wife did not get on at all well together: 'At first we could not even look at one another, but now we are good friends; when I go out to work and come back tired my wife has food ready for me and looks after me; then I love her and think to myself 'this is my wife,' and I am pleased in my belly.' It may be noticed that the belly is considered to be the seat of the emotions.
>
> All ceremonial occasions among the Lepchas—birth, marriage and death, religious ceremonies, exorcism, and civil consultations—are marked by the consumption of extra quantities of food and drink. Even the most solemn religious ceremonies are turned into picnics... When I tried to get some of the best adjusted Lepchas to talk about their own early lives they replied by giving me lists of menus.[118]

It might be of interest to note that while organising for accommodation in Dzongu, the first household that was approached said that they could not support an outsider because they might not be able to provide proper food.

Beef, pork, chicken, mutton and to a lesser extent fish, is consumed on occasions, as meat and especially beef and pork is greatly relished by the Lepchas of Dzongu. But the consumption of beef is being lately discouraged by the Lamas (even though they might eat beef themselves), and a number of Rongs, especially women, have given up eating beef. This is perhaps a mixed influence of Lamaism, Nepali Hindu labourers coupled with the mainstream Hindu belief that it is a sin to eat beef. Donmit Lepcha, married in the Passingdang *busti,* gave up eating beef, as she had to perform the Laxmi *puja* in the absence of her mother-in-law.[119] She has not eaten beef again as, "Once you give up something, it is a sin to come back to it." Her mother-in-law too does not eat beef. The men in the family, however, felt that women give up beef because of the affection they feel towards their cattle. Hunting as a regular means of obtaining meat has declined in Dzongu. In fact it is clear from Gorer's accounts that hunting has not been commonly practised among the Lepchas since the 1930s.[120]

Rongs do not use many spices in the preparation of food. Salt, chillies and locally grown turmeric are the spices used in everyday cooking, though packaged spices are now also brought from the market and used on special occasions and especially in the preparation of meat. Most Lepchas do not consume any sugar and, in fact, do not even store sugar in their homes. They drink salted tea without milk, although some milk is added to the salted tea when it is available. Dr. Bhutia, the doctor in Dzongu, says that the high consumption of salt among the Lepchas is a chief cause for blood pressure related health problems among the Lepchas. A substantial amount of energy and time is also devoted to the preparation of intoxicants like *chi* and *roxy* and these are prepared in every household.

Rice is prepared in a variety of ways: boiled in water and consumed with vegetables, meat or other seasoning. The rice prepared for children is boiled and ground and made into a pudding. Other cereals like wheat, maize and millet are eaten as well. Buckwheat, wheat or millet is ground manually in stone-grinders and kneaded to make dough which is then baked on the cooking stones or griddle. Barley or buckwheat bread is eaten along with vegetable like beans and *kuskus,* a local variety of squash, or with meat on special occasions.

Snacks, also called *khaaja*, after the popular Nepali usage, are not commonly eaten by the Lepchas as they seldom eat between meals. However, munching on snacks is becoming increasingly popular in the larger *busties* which have shops that store chips, biscuits, instant noodles and soft-drinks. However, these consumer patterns have yet not crept in the smaller and more remote *busties* that do not have these stores and Rongs here mainly live off their traditional diet. Traditionally, the Lepchas prepare snacks called *maazen*, made from rice flour and ghee, which are still prepared and savored occasionally with tea and relished by children. Puffed rice with some crisps are another popular snack and offered to guests and Lamas with *chi* or tea. The consumption of puffed rice is perhaps a Nepali influence and sackfulls of puffed rice are purchased for events like funerals and marriages. The Lepchas also prepare Tibetan snacks like *momos* and *thukpa* occasionally. With the opening up of shops in a number of *busties*, an increasing number of children are becoming acquainted with foreign snacks. The most popular among them are Wai-Wai noodles, Maggi noodles, Kurkure and Coke. The popularity of Coke seems to have soured in Dzongu, as well as in the rest of Sikkim, with the advertisement campaign depicting Bollywood star Amir Khan as a Nepali.

It is of interest to observe that the richer people in Dzongu seem to indulge their children a great deal when it comes to buying snacks from shops. In fact, in the absence of markets within close access, the consumption of snacks is almost seen as a status symbol, as otherwise, there are few external factors that can distinguish the poor from the rich. The older Rongs, however, do not favour the growing consumerist habits of the younger Lepchas and consider the mass consumption of packaged snacks an unhealthy habit and a waste of money. Another setback in this pattern of consumption is the influx of waste plastic and aluminium in spite of the ban imposed on plastic in the region. Like much of Sikkim, Dzongu has no proper method of disposing waste; and the Lepchas have taken to either burning plastic waste or simply throwing it down the unsuspecting brooks, glens and mountains. The Rongs are oblivious of the toxins released in the atmosphere by burning plastic. The field NGO in Dzongu, MLAS, too, unfortunately, seems unaware of this detail and, in fact, encourages people to burn plastic instead of throwing it away.

Intoxicants like *chi* are prepared and consumed on a regular basis by the Lepchas. *Chi*, though only mildly inebriating, is more intoxicating than *tumba* and is prepared by the distillation of millet and in its absence may be prepared with wheat, maize or rice in large copper vessels. Millet in Dzongu is almost exclusively grown for making *chi*, the local beer. It has a pleasant mildly sweet flavour and is prepared by fermented *kodo* or millet for a period of about 10 days. Millet is washed in cold water, soaked in hot water and a fermenting agent, *pho*, extracted from a local herb is applied, though readymade yeast brought from the market is commonly used for the purpose. The process of fermentation takes about a week. Once fermented, the millet is served in bamboo containers and hot water is poured on the seeds and consumed with great relish by the Lepchas. The freshly prepared *chi* is sipped with a bamboo straw. At times, *chi* is also flavoured with tapioca roots and on ceremonial occasions, some grains of rice are sprinkled on top of the millet.

The potency of *chi* depends upon the number of times of distillation. *Chi* is also prepared from white tapioca tubers. The tubers are chopped and placed in a bamboo container for 10 to 15 days, in water or a stream. The chopped bits are then sun-dried and boiled in water till cooked. The boiled tubers are then fermented for two days with yeast. The mixture is then transferred into large pots and consumed after 10 to 15 days.

Course of Meal

The Lepchas consume a rather frugal diet on a daily basis and consume only two simple meals a day. The first meal is eaten in the morning at about 8 a.m. In the evening, when the Lepchas return from their fields, they start with the evening tea and at about 7 p.m., eat the second meal of the day. Meals mainly consist of buckwheat bread eaten with a very spicy chutney made of locally grown round chillies and tomatoes and a drink of *chi*; rice is also consumed with vegetables or pulses. A fried dish made from mixing corn dough with vegetables, chillies, or meat on occasions, is also prepared. Bread made of ground corn is also commonly eaten by the Lepchas of Dzongu. The diet differs from season to season but dry and wet rice is a constant factor. Pounded and roasted rice is boiled and eaten with vegetables, chillies or meat. Maize or barley cooked similarly may also substitute rice.

On special occasions, the Lepchas prepare a bread of millet, spread with butter and topped with pieces of fried meat, chilli and vegetables. This bread is then rolled and boiled in water. This dish is, of course, washed down with a drink of *chi*. The second ceremonial dish is made up of maize prepared in a similar manner and eaten with a cup of tea. Steamed pork served on a banana leaf is another ceremonial dish and is a mark of respect for the one being served. Today, however, on special occasions and feasts, Rongs eat a meal that consists of rice, vegetables, meat (preferably beef or pork), pickles and fried *papad*. *Paan* and betel nut, perhaps an influence of the Marwaris, is also relished after a good meal. A number of Rongs have also taken to chewing betel nut. The nature of serving food too has undergone a shift. Earlier, people would serve every individual personally; today however, the Lepchas have adopted the buffet system for bigger events though, in smaller gatherings, the host still serves food to every individual.

The first morsel of food, or a few drops of drink, from every meal are dedicated to the spirits, as a symbolic gesture of inviting them to share and participate in their meal. Brief prayers are recited and some pieces of food or drink thrown in the air. The ritual, however, is not practised by all Lepchas.

Cooking Practices

The traditional kitchen stove of the Lepchas is a platform of earth on which some large stones are placed as supports for the cooking pot of copper or brass. However, many households have adopted the more fuel-efficient Bhutia stoves that are built slightly raised from the ground and have two openings; the opening on the side is for the firewood while the one on top is for the cooking pot. The government has also supplied the Lepcha in Dzongu with gas and burners in an effort to discourage the cutting of wood for fuel. This is a novelty for the Lepchas and most families only use the gas on occasions, as firewood is aplenty and they are not used to gas. Perhaps this may be illustrated by the example that in one house, the inhabitants had kept the gas inside the house in a room on perhaps the nicest table they possessed and not in the kitchen.

Earthenware utensils are not made locally and therefore not in use by the Lepchas. Water is stored in copper vessels as well and transported in long hollow bamboos or pipes though many houses now have a tap, installed by the government, for easy supply of water. A wooden urn and wooden utensils are used for storing liquids. Large baskets are used for keeping dry goods. Traditionally, big leaves are used instead of plates but today most Lepcha households possess a few wooden plates. Some Lepcha households also have a handful of China and metal dishes and containers. Circular grindstones or mortar and pestle are kept adjacent to homes for husking and grinding of grains.

Food is cooked on firewood gathered from the forests. There seems to be no apparent shortage of firewood in Dzongu. Cow-dung is used as manure and not as fuel by the Lepchas.

The Lepchas have also taken to drinking alcoholic beverages and beer from outside. Danny Denzongpa brewery in Sikkim produces a fine lager, Dansberg, while its more potent counterpart is aptly called Hit! And, today, it can easily be said that the young Lepchas of Dzongu (and much of Sikkim) prefer being Hit. These beers are even served in Dzongu during ceremonial functions and funerals, as an increasing number of people are abandoning *chi* in favour of Danny's strong brew.

Largely, it may be said that the Lepchas of Dzongu still subsist on homegrown food, which is enhanced partially by gathering of vegetables and fruits from the abounding forests. The purchasing of grains, cereals and vegetables from the market is still seen as a rather foreign concept for a majority of the Rongs and is done only when necessary. Salt, oil and some other articles of necessity, however, are brought from the market.

ANIMALS AND BIRDS

Observation reveals the close association between man and animal in the Lepcha society. Their mythology aptly reflects this relationship and the Lepcha folklore is replete with tales exhibiting the Lepcha affinity with animals and birds. Given the geographical isolation of Dzongu, and the close proximity to the abounding wilderness, the Rongs initially hunted animals for food and used their skin for warmth against the cold. Gradually, with the shift to settled cultivation and domestication of animals, the fauna in the region played a more significant role in the socio-religious life of the Rongs, as most ceremonies and rituals accompanied an animal sacrifice.

Rituals are important to the Lepcha sense of well-being and Rongs were known to incur much of their debt to obtain animals for sacrifice. Ownership of a large number of animals was considered a symbol of wealth as well as a source of sustenance. A household with 10 to 20 oxen was considered wealthy. Gorer writes,

> By far the most important animal is oxen[121]; they are still the chief signal of wealth... Their meat is the most esteemed and at important feasts, or if a person wants to make a display, it is always an ox which is killed. They are never used as beasts of burden (no animals are so used) but occasionally for ploughing; a certain amount of milk and butter is got from milch-cows. Only the most savage bulls are castrated. Cows are not mated and no pedigrees are kept.

Today, animals and animal products also constitute a significant source of secondary income for the Lepchas; thus, animals have now acquired an important role in their monetary life as well. Animal husbandry and minor trading like the selling of eggs, fowl and meat are important trading and exchange resources employed by the Lepchas. With the impact of Lamaism and the world outside, there is a perceivable fall not only in the frequency of animal sacrifice but in that of rituals and ceremonies as well.[122] Even so, the ceremonial value of animals continues to be significant for the Rongs and important ceremonies like marriage and death are seldom solemnised without animal exchange or sacrifice.

The Lepchas domesticate a variety of animals like cows, bulls, goats, fowl, pigs, dogs and cats. The Tholung family also owns a sizeable number of Yaks and some horses. The use of chemical fertilisers in agriculture started in Dzongu in the 70s and cattle are still kept for valuable draught power and manure for the fields. Cows are milked and bulls are employed for ploughing fields. A man with oxen was traditionally considered rich among the Lepchas and a bull sacrifice is still a symbol of esteem and wealth. Goats do not carry the same prestige but are reared for their meat but not their milk. They are fed on salt and at times maize. Pigs found here belong to a wild Himalayan species and are kept in small sties outside of their homes. Pigs are fed on the remains of *chi*, chaff, kitchen spoils and *arum* leaves. They are domesticated for their meat and sacrifice and are said to be the only domestic animals killed for food as Lepchas relish pork. Dogs are tamed to keep a watch on wild animals and cats to control rodents. Poultry birds are kept in most Lepcha houses for their eggs and meat, while fowls are utilised for their meat and are commonly sacrificed for Mun rituals in Dzongu. Fowls live in a wooden structure, above the raised beam of the house, safe from the reach of wild animals. During the day, they are left free in the yard and fed on grain from the winnowing baskets and querns; at night, they are secured in a basket or inside the homes.

The killing of birds is not of much consequence among the Lepchas and young boys sometimes kill birds with locally made catapults as a pastime. Lepcha legends mention how boys would carry back dead birds for their mothers as presents. This has its practical advantage as the birds are stored by the mothers and used during Mun rituals.

The Lepchas were known for their expertise in fishing but today, the practice of fishing too has faced a setback in the everyday culture of the Lepchas. This is ironic considering the plentiful availability of fish in the copious rivers and waterbodies in and around Dzongu. Among others, this could be a consequence of the various taboos imposed on fish-eating on members of certain *putso* or clans and *busties* in Dzongu. Lepchas that belong to the *putsos* Hee-yam, Hee-mo and Hee-youngming are barred from eating fish from the Ling-do Lake in Dzongu.

Fishing is practised as a leisure activity; children and young men can often be commonly spotted fishing in the rivers that fringe Dzongu. Fishing is also popular during picnics—the favourite activity of the young and old Rongs alike. The Lepchas use nets, traps and fishing poles to catch fish. Bamboo traps are placed near green banks of waterbodies. The nets are made of cotton or *sisnoo* fibres. The also use the *hyren*, a line made by fixing a piece of wood at its end. The piece of wood swallowed by the fish sticks in its throat, thereby killing it. Fish is also caught by diverting water streams and clearing up the dried-up water channels. Fishing rod and line, *humsa sunli*, is also used. Dried fish can be found stored in almost every Lepcha household as it is an essential accoutrement in the offerings to supernaturals.

The Hee-youngming *putso* can use the water of the lake while people from other *putso*s living in Hee-gyathang can even eat the fish. Ant holes are deemed sacred in the Hee-yongming *putso*. In case of diseases, these people make an offering of rice to the pond and rice and maize to ant holes.

When children are old enough, they are traditionally given a small piece of land, and some animals, like chicken, calves or piglets, to feed and take care of. This instills the feeling of responsibility amongst children at an early age and these animals are considered their property and any income generated from them is kept for the child. For girls, the income was often used to buy them jewellery and clothes and after marriage, a girl is allowed to take her animals to her new house as a part of her dowry. In this manner, all the family members are given the feeling of relative economic independence and responsibility from a tender age. The practice still prevails among Lepchas today though it is perhaps not as commonplace, and children can be observed to lay a certain emphasis of ownership and attachment with their animals.

The killing of animals by women and Lamas is strictly prohibited. Furthermore, it is considered a sin to consume an animal killed by a woman. If, by mistake, a woman does kill an animal, she has to perform purification rites conducted by a Lama, and make offerings to the monastery. Lamas too cannot kill animals and have to ask a lay family member to do the deed. Otherwise, anyone is asked to butcher the animal and was traditionally given six to seven kilograms of meat from the crotch of an ox, or a smaller portion from a pig. In case the animal he slaughters was a chicken, his remuneration was in the form of a drink of *chi*. Today, except in ceremonial occasions, animals are usually slaughtered by the Nepali labourers in Dzongu.

The Lepchas perform ceremonies to mollify the supernatural spirit of Zomola Rum in case of infertility or the spread of disease in animals, and offer buttermilk and cheese, and light fires in three vessels and recite prayers. It is of significance to observe that even though the incident of animal sacrifice has come down among the Lepchas, the preparation of *lofit*[123] remains mandatory in every Mun ritual. This implies that dead fish and birds are a prerequisite to conduct even the simplest Mun ceremony.

With the aid of the Department of Animal Husbandry, the Lepchas in Dzongu today breed a superior quality of animals as compared to their ancestors. The department distributes hybrid cows to households based on the recommendations given by Panchayats. Veterinary services are also accessible, even though the distances in Dzongu do not make such exercises short of an ordeal, and apart from health services the Animal Husbandry Department also conveniences feeds, insemination facilities, castration of bulls, pigs and goats. A qualified vet has been stationed in Heegyathang while a veterinary dispensary has been installed in the *busti* of Tingvong in Upper Dzongu. The Department of Fisheries has also established fisheries in Dzongu with an endeavour to encourage the production of fish for the purpose of commerce. A fish farm has been set up in Heegyathang and a fish demonstration farm in the *busti* of Lingdem in Dzongu for enhancing seed production activities.

ENVIRONMENTAL UNDERSTANDING

The lifestyle of the Lepchas of Dzongu illustrates a way of life that is highly receptive and sensitive to their environment. This can be deciphered right from their method of cultivation, house-building techniques, social and religious practices and their superstitions. In fact, it would not be inaccurate to say that successful adaptation and understanding of their environment—forests, weather conditions, topography and geographical location—has played a prime role in ensuring their survival in this difficult territory. The Lepchas of Dzongu possess a deep knowledge of the flora and fauna found in the forests and have a local name for almost every plant found in the area, irrespective of whether the plant has been botanically identified.

In ancient times, with a low human density of population and a plentiful natural resource base, the Lepchas could afford a broad base of subsistence. With the increase in human population and restrictions and decreasing forest area, the Lepchas too turned to domesticating animals and reduced their hunting and gathering activities.

Studies conducted in the region show that the social and cultural patterns of the Lepchas are most closely related to subsistence activities. These in turn are observed to be a response to the environmental features of the area. It is but natural to observe that these people, living in the remote forested landscape in relative isolation from the rest of the world, understand their immediate environment intimately and depend upon it majorly. In ancient times, the Lepchas were nomadic and subsisted mainly on the collection of fruits, roots, tubers, leaves and fishing and hunting. They also practised primitive shifting cultivation with poor and simple technology. Today, things have changed and the locals have moved on to a settled form of agricultural practice enhanced by gathering. Moreover, change has been slow, resulting in an interesting mix of influences from the ancient and the modern. Nonetheless, the environment continues to play a great role in shaping their culture and society. The Lepchas still believe that there can never be a shortage of food, leave alone starvation, as long as the forests exist.

Perhaps the best example to elucidate the depth of environmental understanding of the Lepchas is that Sir Joseph Hooker, the noted English botanist and Superintendent of the celebrated Kew Gardens, conducted the first study of the flora and fauna of Sikkim, in 1848-49, with the assistance of the culturally trained botanists the Lepchas. They already had local names for perhaps nearly all the trees, flowers, grasses, ferns, beasts and birds, and, what's more, could even identify different genera of the flora and fauna of the region in an instant. Hooker's findings from his expeditions with the Lepchas were published as the *Himalayan Journals*, and continue to rank among the most comprehensive and authoritative listings of the botanical treasures of the state till date. Kotturan writes,

> Perhaps it is their life in the mountains that has made the Lepchas so strong. This again gives them a marvelous understanding of the different strains of flowering plants, of the birds and butterflies that their dwellings abound in.[124]

Their knowledge systems and lifestyle also reveal that their expertise on the life in the forest is not limited to just edible species.

Originally, the Lepchas were part-animists and worshipped the spirits of the mountains, forests and rivers; perhaps a direct and natural outcome of their surroundings. Later, however, in keeping with the influences from the outside world, they integrated their indigenous religion with Lamaism. Gradual westernisation and influence of the mainstream Indian culture coupled with the substantial Nepali presence in the state has evolved a generation of Rongs that exhibits a cultural amalgam of all these influences. Gradual changes and modernisation has somewhat dulled the authority of the Rongs on their natural world. They no longer depend upon the forest the way their ancestors did, and this gradual moving away has naturally resulted in a loss of environmental knowledge that is perhaps irrecoverable. This may perhaps be best elucidated by taking the changes in their knowledge systems of medicine, weather forecasting, arts and crafts and agricultural practices, among others, into account. Studies also reveal that just within the sphere of agriculture, the number of varieties of crops grown, like *zomal* or dry rice and paddy, have witnessed a sharp decline in terms of the number of varieties grown. Accounts of scholars reveal that at least five different varieties of dry rice and 26 varieties of wet rice were planted in Dzongu around the 1930s. Today, however, the Lepchas of Dzongu mainly plant only two to three different varieties of paddy, while the cultivation of dry rice has seen almost a complete disappearance in the reserve save for some of the remote precipitous hamlets. Most of the traditional varieties have also been replaced by high-yielding hybrid breeds, even though the Rongs acknowledge the superior flavour of the local varieties of crops. Evidently, an effort needs to be made by the agricultural department to preserve the indigenous varieties of crops and stop further extinction of plant varieties.

Development and Change

There is a proverb in Sikkim that a Rong is like a brass pot that can be used by all households. The Lepchas are known to be receptive to changes brought about by different contacts from the outside world. Insecurity of food supplies and their shy mannerism and nature, however, have been stated as the major factors that have defined their attitude towards change and growth.

Apart from the Bhutia influence, perhaps the chief influences of the outside world in the lives of the Lepchas of Dzongu was the introduction of the immigrant Nepali labourers. The immigrants come from a more urbanised area to the reserve in search of short-term work and monetary gain. The influx of influences from the modern world and people, coupled with exposure to the media, among the relatively isolated Lepchas has resulted in a change of attitude among the Lepchas. Today, the Rongs may act in a manner not typically in accordance with their age-old traditions of the greater common good. The difference between the rich and the poor is also gradually increasing.

After the amalgam of Sikkim into the Indian Union, the government of Sikkim, along with the Central Government, has launched various schemes and programmes to facilitate and improve the standard of living of the Lepchas of Dzongu, and enable them to be a greater part of the Indian mainstream. Government-sponsored schemes in the field of education, health, economy, agriculture and animal husbandry, among others, have been successfully implemented in the reserve. Given the nature of remoteness, culture and geography of the Lepchas of Dzongu, however, this has been no easy task and a lot yet remains to be accomplished, especially in the field of education and health in the reserve. The education department has opened up a number of schools in the area. There is one Senior Secondary School in Heegyathang, three secondary schools in Lingdong, Lingthem and Tingvong, three junior high schools and 13 primary schools; with a total 41 graduate teachers in Dzongu. A number of adult education centres have also been set up in the area.

The Lepchas of Dzongu today have access to a range of facilities and benefits. There is one PHC or Primary Health Centre in Passingdang; child welfare centres have also been set up in the reserve. However, the Lepchas have to go to Mangan when in need of hospital facilities. Earlier, a doctor from Mangan would visit Dzongu from time to time, but now one resident doctor has been permanently stationed in Dzongu at the PHC in Passingdang. Maternity and child welfare centres, run under the supervision of a child development programme officer, have also been established. Even so, many of the Lepchas continue to depend upon Muns or Lamas for medical and supernatural assistance.

The Department of Agriculture has set up nurseries and a research centre to check the viability of growing new crops. The agricultural, horticultural and animal husbandry sectors have recorded significant progress. Planting of new varieties and fruits like orange and apple is on the rise and farmers are more forthcoming in planting high-yielding varieties of grain. A veterinary dispensary has also been set up and a vet posted permanently in the reserve. The Forest Department ensures the safekeeping of the reserve forests, and regular surveys and demarcations are conducted and activities like poaching, overgrazing and clearing of trees is kept under check.

It must be mentioned that the topography of Dzongu and the distribution of population across this formidable landmass makes it difficult for the Lepchas to access the various facilities now available in the reserve. Take the example of roads. The construction of jeepable roads is of fundamental importance towards the development of Dzongu. The North Sikkim highway is subject to frequent landslides. For this reason, until some years back the highway was open only a few months in the year. However, this had little impact on the lives of the locals who made the long and arduous journey to Mangan on foot, much like their ancestors did. Today, the situation has changed as the road is kept open throughout the year, and the inhabitants of Dzongu no longer walk the distance to Mangan but use the daily morning jeep service to get to the district headquarters. Then again, it would be incorrect to assume that this odyssey has become a simple exercise. It is important to note that much of Dzongu continues to remain cut off from roads and the inhabitants of these areas have to walk for hours on end to reach the nearest road head to avail of the jeep service.

This mode of transport is expensive as well. The one-way hour-long trip from Passingdang, among the nearest *busti*es from Mangan, costs Rs 30. The nearest jeepable roads too are in a state of disrepair with long distances still uncarpeted, rendering them highly risky during the rainy season and difficult to manoeuvre at best. The maintenance of roads was given little impetus in the past decades and the project has only picked up recently after 1983, a startling lag of about 20 years. Remote *busti*es like Sakyong, Pentong, Leek, Lum, parts of Heegyathang and even the populous *busti* of Lingthem, to mention but a few, remain disconnected by road. This perhaps illustrates that though Dzongu might have been 'connected' by road but getting to the nearest road-head for people in much of Dzongu continues to be a laborious task. Indeed, some of the inhabitants of Pentong visit Mangan only as rarely as once a year.

Getting to the holiest shrine in Dzongu—the Tholung Monastery—would make the Vaishno Devi Yatra, or even the Amarnath Yatra seem like a mere trifle. After trudging through the lush paddy fields of Lingyah interspersed with gurgling brooks and waterfalls, come the cardamom rich plantations around the *busti* of Bay. These gradually give way to a boulder-strewn landscape fringed by the torrential Tholung River. But it is wise to keep your eyes on the ground as there are no paved pathways here and a slip could well prove to be fatal. The dark and mysterious upper woodlands of oak, laurels and rhododendron begin shortly after this. The forests are thick with undergrowth and only let some sunlight filter to the ground in patches. Some trees here have hollows that might easily fit in an elephant. The weather conditions are often signified by constant rainfall, and here leeches not only latch on to anything that moves from the undergrowth, but tiger leeches also drop from the trees above. It is a foolish exercise to stop to remove them, for the only assurance of not getting several more firmly attached to your skin is to constantly keep walking. The resting sheds constructed in a few places are the only safe spot to examine the bloody limbs and catch a breath. Encounters with poisonous snakes are not uncommon and one has to constantly keep an eye on where the next step is to be placed. Tholung lies in a beautiful valley surrounded by high mountain peaks and waterfalls and since there is no supermarket here, rations, along with sleeping bags, have to be carried all the way up.

This is a day's journey for the hardy Lepchas, but even the adventurous outsiders wisely break the journey at Bay or take a small diversion and halt at the breathtaking Pentong. Indeed, there are few villages as picturesque as Pentong, this remote hamlet in the Himalayas. The uphill climb is well worth the extra effort just for the stupendous vistas to be enjoyed here, but more importantly, Pentong also allows a glimpse of a people and life reminiscent of a time long gone by. It is here, as in some other remote *hamlets* of Dzongu, that remnants of the Lepcha culture, now only available in the accounts of scholars like Gorer, may be experienced with a measure of bliss. The handful of households here live their lives together in a community system representative of the unique Lepcha traditions. There is little cardamom grown here and the influx of immigrant labourers is rare. People get up at the crack of dawn and spend their days toiling and sweating in the fields, taking brief breaks for a laugh and a song. *Chi* is thoroughly enjoyed after the day's labour and feasts are marked by gay abandon and much jest. Simplicity and charm are to be tasted here in epic proportions. Women are smiling and graceful; men are strong; and children are forever free. Time moves lazily, and days go past in an unhurried haze, like the flapping wings of a white Himalayan bird. There is little care here for quotas or power generators. And, unlike much of Dzongu today, the Bongthing here is still every man's king. Like much of India, Dzongu too continues to live and thrive in different time frames and ideologies.

An effort has been made to uplift the Lepchas, and ensure that the transition does not result in the extinction of the rich cultural heritage of this historic race. However, these endeavours have only met with partial success and the lack of authoritative documentation and research available on the Lepchas is indeed a grave void. However, it would be incorrect to solely blame the government, or indeed the Lepchas for the choices they might have made. Change being perhaps the only constant, democratic ethos disallows a people to be examined as museum relics and forced into isolation. Indeed, few aspects of their ideology today reinforces themselves as strongly as their desire to be a part of the bigger picture and participate in the mainstream. The impetus of keeping the culture of the Lepchas alive, perhaps to some extent, lies with the Lepchas themselves. The local NGO run under the able leadership of President Namgyal Lepcha has done some commendable work in the direction and perhaps some of the most significant measures to revive their culture have been undertaken by this small organisation.

The Lepchas are classified as a tribal people by the Indian Union and are thus allowed a quota of reserved seats. However, the state government has committed a remarkable blunder by clubbing the Lepchas together with the elite Bhutias under the same category. The result is that the privileged Bhutias occupy the majority of the available quota seats leaving the Lepchas high and dry. The Lepcha association rightfully demands that the seats be shared equally by the Bhutias and Lepchas, but no steps have so far been taken towards this shift.

'Progress' also comes to town in the guise of the Teesta Hydel Project. The National Hydel Project Corporation and the Central Water Commission have started the construction of a dam in Legship, and the Lepchas claim that the land of a few Lepchas has been forcefully confiscated in return for compensations they do not want. The land of some Lepchas in the *busti* of Lum has also been snatched from them. This has also resulted in the establishment of homes and bases of employees of the NHPC within the 'Reserve' of the Lepchas. A population of outsiders is soon to be stationed in the *busties* of Passingdang, Heegyathang, Lingzyah and Kahim. These steps not only violate the premises of the Lepcha Reserve but are believed to encroach on the boundaries of the Kangchendzonga National Park as well. Passing references are also made by some Lepchas on some prostitutes believed to be operating in the area around Dikchu and lower Dzongu, owing to the beginnings of the controversial Teesta Hydel Project. The Lepchas also believe that changing the course of rivers and meddling with stones brings grave misfortunes and are deeply unhappy with the activities of the Teesta Project.

"This is the second time you haven't replied to my chat message", said a Lepcha girl to another, exchanging pleasantries at the picnic organised for the people in government service in Dzongu, by the MLA, at Namprikdang. Two internet centres have been set up in the Reserve and the Central Government has recently supplied about a dozen computers to all the secondary and senior secondary schools in Dzongu, under a scheme launched by the president of India. This implies that even though the students might not have roads to go to school, they can still ride on the information highway on their rickety bicycles.

Notes

1. Population statistics are taken from the 2001 census report.
2. *Lepcha: My Vanishing Tribe* by A.R. Foning.
3. *Lepchas and their Heritage* by Tapan Chattopadhyay, p. 42.
4. *Lepchas of Sikkim* by Geoffrey Gorer, p. 148.
5. *Lepchas of Sikkim* by Geoffrey Gorer, pp. 161-62.
6. *Lepchas of Sikkim* by Geoffrey Gorer, p. 336.
7. *Lepchas of Sikkim* by Geoffrey Gorer, p. 153.
8. Geoffery Gorer's study of the Lepchas was conducted in the 1930s.
9. *Lepchas of Sikkim* by Geoffrey Gorer, p. 154.
10. *Lingthem Revisited. Social Change in a Lepcha Village of North Sikkim* by Rip Roshinna Gowloog, p. 81.
11. *The Lepchas of Sikkim* by Geoffrey Gorer, p. 160.
12. *Lepchas of Sikkim* by Geoffrey Gorer, p. 322.
13. This information was given by Cheddamu Lepcha, 81, of the Sankalang busti.
14. *Lingthem Revisited: Social Change in a Lepcha Village of North Sikkim* by Rip Roshinna Gowloog, pp. 36-37.
15. *Lepchas and their Heritage* by Tapan Chattopadhyay, p. 41.
16. *Ecology Culture and Change: Tribals of Sikkim Himalayas* by Veena Bhasin, 1983.
17. The information on the socio-political system of Dzongu and especially the council of Kyoung Shezum was given by the Panchayat member Ugan Lepcha, 24, of Passingdang *busti*. I have not found any published reference on the above-mentioned council.

18. The above-mentioned figures were given to me by Mika Lepcha and Namgyal Lepcha of Passingdang and Leek busties, and other Lepchas in Dzongu.
19. For details, see the section on Ceremonies and Festivals.
20. *Lepchas of Sikkim* by Geoffrey Gorer, p. 181.
21. *Lepchas of Sikkim* by Geoffrey Gorer, pp. 182-83.
22. *Lepchas of Sikkim* by Geoffrey Gorer, p. 182.
23. *Lepchas and their Heritage* by Tapan Chattopadhyay, pp. 29-30.
24. *Lepcha: My Vanishing Tribe* by A.R. Foning.
25. *Lepchas and their Heritage* by Tapan Chattopadhyay, p. 30.
26. *Lepchas and their Heritage* by Tapan Chattopadhyay, pp. 30, 33.
27. *Lepchas of Sikkim* by Geoffrey Gorer, pp. 232, 234.
29. *Lepchas of Sikkim* by Geoffrey Gorer, p. 215.
30. *Ecology Culture and Change: Tribals of Sikkim Himalayas* by Veena Bhasin.
31. *Lingthem Revisited* by Rip Roshina Gowloog, pp. 114-15.
32. *Lingthem Revisited* by Rip Roshina Gowloog, p. 116.
33. *Lepcha: My Vanishing Tribe* by A.R. Foning.
34. *Lepchas of Sikkim* by Geoffrey Gorer, p. 235.
35. *Lepchas of Sikkim* by Geoffrey Gorer, p. 238.
36. *Lofit* is prepared on a bamboo tray open on one side, which is covered with banana leaves. The tray is lined with three rows of beaten rice on which are placed bits of a dead fish and bird killed by a catapult, ghee, ginger, *chi, lop* or leaves, and lamps which are lit during the ceremony.
37. According to local belief, the origin of the Lepchas is said to be from the Khangchendzonga and its immediate surroundings. But different *putsos* also link their relations to various other mountain peaks that surround their place of habitation. It is not altogether uncommon for more than one *putsos* to worship the same peak and perform an annual sacrifice for the spirit of the mountain. The origin of a *putso* might also be from a waterfall, cave, lake, pond, etc. It is also not considered problematic for more than one *putso* to worship the same source as long as they are not related by blood. During marriages, the bride has to perform the sacrifice of a rooster to the spirit of the groom's *putso*.
38. The detail of the importance of the third day was given by the Bongthing Kenchyok Lepcha of Pentong.
39. *Lepchas of Sikkim* by Geoffrey Gorer, p. 289.
40. *Chi* is especially prepared for the birth ceremony and it is said that it should not be touched before the ritual.
41. Cheddamu Lepcha is known in Dzongu as a woman with an exceptional memory and profound knowledge of the Mun religion.

42. *Kafer lop* is a broad leaf which forms one of the essential accoutrements of the Mun. In the burial ritual, two packages of *kafer lop* containing *chi* and rice are made. One is for three days while the other is for eight days. The Lepchas believe that the soul feels hungry while it is travelling to its destination and burying some essentials along with the body is a custom originating from this belief.
43. *Pushyor lop* is a leaf which is mandatory for all the rituals conducted by a Lepcha priest; hence; the plant can be found not only in the wild but in the garden of almost every Lepcha house in Dzongu.
44. *The Lepchas of Sikkim* by Geoffrey Gorer, p. 450.
45. *The Lepchas of Sikkim* by Geoffrey Gorer, p. 249.
46. *The Lepchas of Sikkim* by Geoffrey Gorer, pp. 280-81.
47. *The Lepchas of Sikkim* by Geoffrey Gorer, pp. 260, 276.
48. *The Lepchas of Sikkim* by Geoffrey Gorer, p. 273.
49. This conversation took place with Mr. N.T. Lepcha, who chairs the Animal Husbandry Department in the Mangan Secretariat.
50. For details see the section on Religion.
51. *Lepchas of Sikkim* by Geoffrey Gorer, p. 263.
52. *Lepchas of Sikkim* by Geoffrey Gorer, p. 283.
53. *Lepchas of Sikkim* by Geoffrey Gorer, p. 308.
54. Gorer's study was conducted in the 1930s.
55. *Lepchas of Sikkim* by Geoffrey Gorer, p. 322.
56. *Lepchas of Sikkim* by Geoffrey Gorer, pp. 317-18.
57. *Lepchas of Sikkim* by Geoffrey Gorer, p. 263.
58. *Lepchas of Sikkim* by Geoffrey Gorer, p. 279.
59. *Lepchas of Sikkim* by Geoffrey Gorer, p. 280.
60. *Lepchas of Sikkim* by Geoffrey Gorer, p. 331.
61. The Tista Hydel Project, if the Lepcha version is to be believed, is not only the cause of some emerging, and rather disturbing, social problems in Dzongu, but is the source of devastations in their economic sphere as well. This view is also backed by some Ngos operating in Sikkim. Sections of the precious 'reserved' land of the Lepchas of Dzongu, and the chief ingredient of their security and wellbeing, is today reportedly being confiscated by the NHPC in lieu of compensations the Lepchas have apparently no wish for. This ironic role of the state, and a reoccurring and unfortunate one in our country, requires imminent study and reactions.
62. *Lepchas and their Heritage* by Tapan Chattopadhyay, p. 65.
63. This resemblance is not very obvious to the lay eye; out of the 56 Lepcha characters, 18 have no parallel in the U-med alphabet,

and, of the 38 signs common to both, over half have very different forms.

64. *Lepchas of Sikkim* by Geoffrey Gorer, pp. 38-39.
65. *Lungten sung* or myth is an omnibus word for fables, fairy-tales, legends and folklore.
66. The information on the script was given by Namgyal and Mika Lepcha of Passingdang and Leek *busties*.
67. The information on the script was given by Namgyal and Mika Lepcha of Passingdang and Leek *busties*.
68. The information on the script was given by Namgyal and Mika Lepcha of Passingdang and Leek *busties*.
69. *Lepchas and their Heritage*, Tapan Chattopadhyay, p. 64.
70. Note by Gen. Mainwaring: In the structure of the Lepcha language I have discovered the system on which I consider, all language is based. By an exegesis which I have, in part, prepared (combined with a diagram showing the rudimental power of letter), the root and true signification of all words in all languages are, at once, apparent.
71. *Lepchas of Sikkim* by Geoffrey Gorer, p. 35.
72. *Lepchas and their Heritage* by Tapan Chattopadhyay, p. 65.
73. Jiroong was a descendant of former slaves. Some generations ago his ancestor, then a small boy, was kidnapped by Bhutanese; but the boy was rescued by the then head of the village. *The Lepchas of Sikkim*, Geoffrey Gorer, p. 43.
74. *The Lepchas of Sikkim*, Geoffrey Gorer, p. 43.
75. *Folktales and Customs of the Lap-chas of Sikkim* by C. de Beauvoir Stocks, from the Journal and Proceedings of the Asiatic Society of Bengal (New Series), Vol. XXI, 1925, No.4.
76. *Lepchas and their Heritage*, Tapan Chattopadhyay, p. 65.
77. *Lingthem Revisited* by Rip Roshina Gowloog, p. 26.
78. George Kotturan is a Lepcha from Darjeeling and has written several books on his tribe including the above-quoted *The Himalayan Gateway – History and Culture of Sikkim*.
79. *Lepchas and their Heritage*, Tapan Chattopadhyay, p. 37.
80. George Kotturan has sourced material for his book *Folk Tales of Sikkim* from the Lepchas in and around Darjeeling. As a result, his account of the Lepcha folklore is different from what the Lepchas of Dzongu are familiar with.
81. Frank Boas, *Tsimsnian Mythology*, 1916.
82. Chattopadhyay explains *tangbor* as the imaginative outflow of a culture in the doma in of thought and language. p. 63.

83. *Lepchas and their Heritage* by Tapan Chattopadhyay, p. 39.
84. In my observation, *Bongthings* and not so much the *Muns* are commonly employed to cure diseases.
85. This information was given by the most respected medicine man of Dzongu, the 71-year-old Tshering Badur Lepcha, of the Leek *busti*.
86. Geoffrey Gorer conducted his research in Lingthem, Dzongu in the 1930s.
87. *Vaidhnath* could be roughly translated as an *ayurvedic* doctor or one who cures diseases with the use of medicinal plants, among other things.
88. This statement can perhaps be verified by the case of one Nepalese labourer who I had heard was taken in the hospital for five months after he broke his thigh-bone. It was said that he continued to be in great pain even after he was discharged from the hospital. This labourer then decided to seek the help of Tshering, who is believed to have cured him completely in a month's time, and now the labourer is reported to be working in the fields as fit as a fiddle.
89. The public health outpost in the Passingdang *busti* of Dzongu is, so far, only reached by a tough climb of about 200 crude steps. The project of connecting the health centre by road, however, has taken off. The only doctor in the entire region Dr. Bhutia says that the climb cannot be termed as pleasant even for the fit. He personally has to ensure he gets back to his house, situated besides the health centre, before dark. Not to mention the effort required to carry his supplies to his home. But the doctor's misfortunes may be termed as mild compared to what the people of the remote areas undergo. Some of the inhabitants of the far-flung Pentong visit Mangan only as rarely as once a year.
90. The nursery in Passingdang was started with the help of MLAS, the local NGO in Dzongu.
91. This information is given purely on the basis of what was reported to me by the people of Dzongu. I have found no other relevant reference to their weather forecasting system.
92. *Lepchas of Sikkim* by Geoffrey Gorer, pp. 212-13.
93. *Lepchas of Sikkim* by Geoffrey Gorer, p. 214.
94. *The Lepchas of Sikkim* by Geoffrey Gorer, p. 65.
95. *The Lepchas of Sikkim* by Geoffrey Gorer, p. 66.
96. *Lepchas of Sikkim* by Geoffrey Gorer, p. 67.
97. *Lepchas of Sikkim* by Geoffrey Gorer, p. 68.

98. *The Lepchas of Sikkim* by Geoffrey Gorer, p. 65.
99. *Ecology Culture and Change: Tribals of Sikkim Himalayas* by Veena Bhasin.
100. The details of construction are presented in the full report.
101. *The Lepchas of Sikkim* by Geoffrey Gorer, pp. 84, 86.
102. *The Lepchas of Sikkim* by Geoffrey Gorer, p. 69.
103. *Lepchas and their Heritage* by Tapan Chattopadhyay, p. 73.
104. *The Lepchas of Sikkim* by Geoffrey Gorer, p. 197.
105. *The Himalayan Journal* by Dr. Joseph Hooker, p. 124.
106. *Lepchas and their Heritage* by Tapan Chattopadhyay, p. 75.
107. *Lepchas and their Heritage* by Tapan Chattopadhyay, pp. 74-75.
108. The details of the dances as well as the Legend of the Hunters were given by Namgyal Lepcha of the Passingdang *busti*.
109. For details on the Story of Origin, refer to Folklore.
110. *The Lepchas of Sikkim* by Geoffrey Gorer, pp. 62-63.
111. *The Lepchas of Sikkim* by Geoffrey Gorer, p. 70.
112. Also, see the Ceremonies section in this report for rituals related to house construction.
113. *The Lepchas of Sikkim* by Geoffrey Gorer, p. 74.
114. *Lepchas of Sikkim* by Geoffrey Gorer, p. 91.
115. *Lingthem Revisited* by Rip Roshina Gowloog, p. 42.
116. *Lingthem Revisited* by Rip Roshina Gowloog, p. 46.
117. *Lingthem Revisited* by Rip Roshina Gowloog, p. 46.
118. *Lepchas of Sikkim* by Geoffrey Gorer, pp. 83-84.
119. Laxmi *puja* is a relatively new phenomenon in Dzongu, and many Lepchas perform a small *puja* at home for the Hindu goddess of wealth, Laxmi, a day before Diwali.
120. *Lepchas of Sikkim* by Geoffrey Gorer, pp. 84-85.
121. The Lepcha cattle have no hump; they resemble small European rather than Indian cattle. They have small horns and every variety and combination of colouring.
122. For details refer to the chapter Religion.
123. *Lofit* is prepared on a bamboo tray open on one side which is covered with banana leaves. The tray is covered with three rows of beaten rice on which are placed bits of a dead fish and bird killed by a catapult, ghee, ginger, *chi*, lop or leaves, and lamps which are lit during the ceremony.
124. *The Himalayan Gateway – History and Culture of Sikkim* by George Kotturan.

Glossary

Addhi Mung — demon of quarrels

Adhia — half

Adik mass — extra month added after 3 years to balance the calendar

Aee-rungpuh — a wooden barrel resembling a tree trunk for housing Himalayan honeybees

A-pil — eight souls of a man six souls of a woman

Asek — bride price

Bahur — sickle

Bhoomkor — Annual Tibet ceremony adopted by Lepcha to ward off sickness

Bhusna — an insect commonly found in the cardamom plantations

Bongthing — senior Lepcha priest

Bree — bridal home

Bri — Marriage feast, when the bridge comes to her husband's home

Bum fork — knife

Chabri-bu — first of seven degrees for a Lama

Che-ne — (1) Lamaist priest.
(2) Lamaist ceremony.

Cher-kem — Offering to devils made either by laymen or Lamas during Lamaist ceremonies: consists of mixed grains

	floating in strained *chi*, which is thrown on to the ground with a wooden spoon to the cry of "Lo Chi-do"- "take this"
Chi	Lepcha beer: made by pouring boiling water on to fermented millet or other grain: drunk hot
Da-floh	a ceremonial dance performed in front of a Lamaist altar.
De Rum	ancestral god who looks after dead Lepchas
a-dum	white
Elaiji nyou	goddess of cardamom
Fung Mung	spirit which causes violent harm to households
Ga-zook	the head, one foreleg and one hindleg of the animal sacrificed by a mun
Ge-long	celibate Lama
Gompa	monastery
Gya-pon	village official: a temporary post
Gye to lung ji rum	ceremony to propitiate the spirit Gye
Hyren	a fishing line with a wooden stick as bait
Ingzong	institutional or group to group friendship
Kafer lop	a broad leaf
Kokyoku	wheat bread
Korhuku	millet bread
Kum bun	a sword
Kuskus	a variety of squash
Kutki, Jata moshi, Chirata,dhoop, kaching	plants commonly used in herbal medicine
a-kut	a symbolical present of a piece of cooked meat, accepted by parents-in-law instead of the bride-price from a poor but otherwise suitable groom.
Kyoung Shezurn	society members
La krong	morning
Layo	sin

Lho paying for help with money

Lhenthop assistance in death ceremonies

Li Rum protective household deity

Lobu, Lyangccho, Ochhom mutual aid groups

Lofit sacrificial offering

Luna ji Mung ceremony to appease a spirit

Lungten Sung mythology

Lungtitchihit Marriage by elopement

Lyang-ganbu village elders

Lyang rum sacrificial ceremony to appeas the fearful supernatural Lyang

Madrum ceremony to mollify hunting goddess

Mandal the head of the village

Maree sung ko chanting of mantras

Mik ka tab a mung ceremony to appease the malicious demon of darkness

Mit Rum ancestral god who looks after dead Lepchas

Moong devil: evilly-disposed supernatural

Mongku buckwheat

Mun a man or woman possessed by the Mun spirit: A priest of the Lepcha religion

Mung a malignant spirit

Mun-then private contemplation in which a Mun enters into communication with a spirit

Munyaam kup a dead spirit

Nam a year

Namaal celebration of the Lepcha new year

Nyom daughter-in-law: bride

Ohlok collective labour

Oong water

Padeem rum faat Ritual performed by Muns and Bongthing, around March-April to retain their powers

Pa-dem man possessed by Padem spirit; similar to but weaker than Mun.

Pa-tyool	'tankard'; a ten-inch section of bamboo with a natural fibrous bottom from which *chi* is drunk
Pho	a fermenting agent
Putso	the patrilineal group
Pushyor lop	a leaf
Rong	Lepcha
Rum	(1) god: benevolently disposed supernatural (2) a mum offering to the gods or devils, in a basket filled with earth, into which are inserted a number of containers of various sorts of food and drink, etc.
Sa gi	Family ceremony for the spirit Padim Rum
Saiak	a day
Sambrange kung	tree observed for weather indications
So nap	night
Sola	evening
Sor moong	violent death
Sheda	monastic school
Suneen	ceremony performed to ward off evil in case of death and other misfortunes
Tak bo thing	an important supernatural personage
Tandong Lho *Rum Faat*	ceremony performed for the deity of Tandong mountain
Tashay Namthar	earliest written text of the Lepchas
Tee lazyee lazum	wooden knitting needle
Thamuyeth	help of cash in death ceremony
Tuksee Rum	god of medicine men
Vyanhram	purification ceremony of new house
Youmi	tax collection official
Zomal	dry rice

Bibliography

Bhasin, Veena, *Ecology, Culture and Change: Tribals of Sikkim Himalayas*, Inter-India Publications, Delhi (1989).

Bhattacharya, P.K., *Aspects of Cultural History of Sikkim*, K.P. Bagchi, Calcutta (1984).

Chattopadhyay, T., *Lepchas and their Heritage*, B.R. Publishers, New Delhi (1990).

Foning, A.R., *Lepcha: My Vanishing Tribe*, Sterling Publishers Pvt. Ltd., New Delhi (1987).

Gorer, Geoffrey, *Himalayan Village: An Account of the Lepchas of Sikkim*. Michael Joseph, London (1938). Reprinted as *The Lepchas of Sikkim*.

Gowloog, R.R., *Lingthem Revisited: Social Change in a Lepcha Village of North Sikkim*, Har Anand Publications, New Delhi (1995).

Kotturan, G., *The Himalayan Gateway – History and Culture of Sikkim*. Sterling Publishers Pvt. Ltd., New Delhi (1983).

Kotturan, G., *Folktales of Sikkim*. Sterling Publishers Pvt. Ltd., New Delhi (1983).

Pallis, Marco, *The Way and the Mountain*, P. Owen (1960).

Salisbury, C.Y., *Sikkim – The Mountain Kingdom*. Hossem and Co., New York (1972).

Sharma, R. and R. Bedi, *Images of Sikkim: The Land, People and Culture*, Rigsum Productions (1983).

Waddel, L.A., *Lamaism in Sikkim* (1973).

Index